Complex Cloth

A Comprehensive Guide
to Surface Design

**FIBER
STUDIO**
PRESS
An Imprint of
That Patchwork Place

Jane Dunnewold

Credits

Editor-in-Chief .... Kerry I. Hoffman
Technical Editor .... Melissa A. Lowe
Managing Editor .... Judy Petry
Copy Editor .... Liz McGehee
Proofreader .... Melissa Riesland
Illustrator .... Laurel Strand
Photographer .... Brent Kane
Text and Cover Designer .... Cheryl Stevenson
Production Assistant .... Claudia L'Heureux

Complex Cloth: A Comprehensive Guide to Surface Design
© 1996 by Jane Dunnewold
That Patchwork Place, Inc., PO Box 118, Bothell, WA 98041-0118 USA

Printed in Hong Kong
01 00 99   6 5 4

Library of Congress Cataloging-in-Publication Data

Dunnewold, Jane,
    Complex cloth : a comprehensive guide to surface design / Jane Dunnewold.
        p.   cm.
      ISBN 1-56477-149-0
      1. Textile design. 2. Textile finishing. I Title.
TT699.D84   1996   96-26494
746—dc20   CIP

MISSION STATEMENT

WE ARE DEDICATED TO PROVIDING QUALITY PRODUCTS AND SERVICES THAT INSPIRE CREATIVITY. WE WORK TOGETHER TO ENRICH THE LIVES WE TOUCH.

That Patchwork Place is a financially responsible ESOP company.

FIBER STUDIO PRESS
An Imprint of
That Patchwork Place

That Patchwork Place®

Dedication

To Zenna and John with love

Acknowledgments

Projects like this are always collaborations in many ways. I would like to thank Ric Collier for his support and encouragement at the Southwest Craft Center. Without it, the idea of complex cloth might never have occurred to me.

The opportunity to work with the staff of That Patchwork Place is a gift. Their dedication to ensuring that every aspect of making a book be the best it can be is inspiring. Special thanks to Kerry Hoffman and Melissa Lowe, who gracefully guided me during the development and production of the manuscript, and Cheryl Stevenson, whose mastery of graphic design and layout truly inspired me.

Without John Carroll, I would never have had the courage to attempt computer literacy. His hours of educational support and the explanations that went with them have changed how I work with words. And the hours of love and entertainment he spent with Zenna while I worked have enriched us all as a family.

Without my dad, Larry Dunnewold, I would never have learned to write.

Beth Kennedy and David Walker collaborated with me on a project based on the idea of complex cloth. Thank you both, for helping me see it was an idea worth sharing.

This project would be nothing without all the wonderful and giving students (and friends) with whom I have had the honor of working. The synergy created in my teaching studio has given my life a buoyancy I could not have experienced any other way. You all know who you are and how our lives have been changed by working together. Thanks to each of you.

And, finally, very special thanks to two most wondrous women: Renita Kuhn, my friend and collaborator, and a talented artist—you believed in me when I could barely believe in myself—and Elinor Palmer Dunnewold, my mother. Creativity and perseverance flowed from your bones into mine. My success is also yours.

Contents

Organizing Chaos by Jane Dunnewold, 1996, San Antonio, Texas, 84" x 54". Cotton and interfacing hand painted with dye. Silk-screened.

For Inspiration

Foreword

In 1992, Jane Dunnewold invited me to teach a workshop in machine appliqué at the Southwest Craft Center in San Antonio, Texas, where she chairs the Surface Design Studio. It was an exciting time for me because it was my first teaching contract that required air travel, and I was decidedly nervous about meeting the expectations of Jane and the students. I will never forget our first meeting or the sense of instant familiarity and friendship we shared. Perhaps this was because Jane and I have similar backgrounds—we both have degrees in religion and managerial restaurant experience, and we both taught ourselves what we know about art and fiber. For whatever reasons, our friendship was an instant success and has grown despite the miles separating our homes and studios.

I have returned to SCC twice more to teach workshops, as well as to participate in a collaborative project with Jane and Austin, Texas, artist Beth Kennedy. Jane had the initial inspiration for what has become a three-year collaborative project, entitled "Dialogues from the Heart." Throughout the collaboration, Jane encouraged a spirit of experimentation and playfulness. She created the only kind of environment that serious artists require—one where it is unquestionably safe to think and dream, to experiment and make mistakes, to share and cry and laugh, and where self-expression is nurtured and celebrated. In short, Jane provided for Beth and me a "home" befitting a family of collaborative artists.

I recount the above to emphasize that Jane's willingness to share her knowledge and her ability to inspire others extends to all who come to her with a desire to work with fabric and to use it as a means of creative self-expression. Her students will assuredly attest to this fact. Jane is passionate about fabric, respecting its delicate yet powerful qualities and supporting its integrity. Jane's driving goal has been to "make cloth sing." And sing it does!

Complex Cloth is more than a book about techniques and processes. It is an invitation to Jane's studio. What you will find here is comfortable reading and friendly instructions for making each length of fabric your own. Everyone will try the same procedures, but it seems impossible that the end cloth will look the same.

Emerging fiber artists thirst to separate themselves from the glut of derivative work produced today. Artists need methods and techniques they can adapt to their individual creative personalities. I believe *Complex Cloth* has the potential to yield that result.

Jane inspires within me the need to look more deeply into the motivations that guide and sustain my work. What I have learned from her has helped my work become more meaningful and rich. It is my hope that you will learn from and be enriched by this book. More importantly, may you be inspired to create new and interesting fabrics that bear the imprint of your unique and creative gifts. Lastly, may your fabrics not only become more beautiful and expressive, but may they, like Jane's, sing!

David Walker
Artist and Quiltmaker
Cincinnati, Ohio

Preface

Complex Cloth evolved as an idea over a long period of time. In March 1990, Ric Collier, president of the Southwest Craft Center in San Antonio, Texas, hired me to create the Surface Design Studio. Faced with the task of developing courses that could be offered to students as part of an ongoing curriculum, I inventoried what I knew. My degree is in psychology and religion, and I taught myself most of what I know about textiles. Suddenly, I became aware of what I *didn't* know!

The first semester, we offered a course titled "Introduction to Surface Design." I spent the week prior to each class learning to do the techniques I would teach the students. Fortunately, my students were clever and enthusiastic, and at the end of the semester, I knew much more than I could have ever learned on my own.

I have never looked back. When Susan I. Jones from That Patchwork Place approached me about publishing *Complex Cloth*, I was thrilled! I know you will find these techniques as exciting and accessible as I did when I first set out to master them. Be willing to experiment—adopt a playful attitude and in no time you will be creating complex cloth of your own.

Introduction

It is possible to create fabric of great depth and complexity—what I call "complex cloth"—simply by beginning with white fabric and layering surface-design processes like dyeing, painting, bleaching, and foiling over one another until a pleasing result is achieved. These and other surface design processes are the focus of this book.

I arrived where I am now, and at the beauty of complex cloth, by a very circuitous route. Unlike my three sisters, who moved gracefully through their childhood experiences and smoothly into careers as lawyers and a psychologist, I have always bumbled and bounced. I spent my early adult years getting what I now think of as real-life experience—waitressing, teaching kindergarten, managing an apartment complex, and finally, co-owning and managing a restaurant. Textile arts were what I did in my spare time. The jobs all worked out. I certainly learned a great deal from them, but they weren't right for me. I kept trying to figure out what was missing. At one particularly low point, my maternal grandmother pulled me to her and said, "We all have a purpose, honey. Sometimes it just takes us longer than other people to figure out what it is." I can't say I knew at that point things would work out for me, but the seed of faith had been planted.

Not long after, I was hired to teach at the Southwest Craft Center. I was surrounded by enthusiastic students every week, and I felt buoyed by their excitement. Each time I taught the introductory class,

I found I had picked up something new to share. But the relationship between the techniques was missing. How, I wondered, can we use all those techniques together? How can we make the cloth sing? I challenged myself to use as many of the processes I taught as possible on one length of cloth, and the idea of complex cloth was born.

I have produced more than three hundred lengths of cloth—from one to six yards each—since those first experiments, and I have never been bored. Each length is unique. Sometimes several are related as a series, and sometimes a piece stands on its own. I have shared my cloth with other artists who have created clothing, some of which is represented in this book. The lengths I could not bear to cut up eventually became art quilts—a satisfying adventure I might never have undertaken if I hadn't made the cloth. I have seen students come to class at a complete loss as to what to do or why they were there and leave triumphant at the end of a semester with their completed complex cloth garment slung over a shoulder. I finally found my place. Grandmother was right.

Aside from technique, which anybody can learn if they have the right book or a good teacher, I believe success relies on the cultivation of inspiration. I tell my students, as I am telling you, to look up, look down, look all around. The world is a miraculous and fascinating place, and ideas are everywhere. I keep a journal with quotes and observations. I pick up junk from the street, I

plant flowers, and I try to see my world in a fresh new light every single day. Design is all around you, and it is usually free for the taking. You may make wondrous cloth based on what you learn in this book, but if your eyes are newly opened to the world around you, we will have both succeeded beyond these limited pages.

7

How to Use This Book

In writing *Complex Cloth*, I have tried to provide you with a clear guide, not only to specific processes, but also to the order in which they can be used. These chapters began as notes for my students, and I have tried to maintain the feeling of hands-on teaching in these pages. As you read and work, it may be helpful to keep some things in mind.

Surface design, the area of textile arts in which complex cloth resides, is a burgeoning field. The processes and materials available today didn't exist twenty years ago. Just as there are countless new products on the market, there are countless ways to use them. It would take more than one book to outline every possible product and process.

Complex Cloth describes techniques and a system of layering that have worked for me. But remember, there are other approaches; be open to them. Use the materials I describe here as I suggest you use them, but be willing to experiment. The field of surface design advances because brave souls try combinations and materials no one else has considered. If you encounter a technique I have not discussed, consider finding out more about it so you can include it in your repertoire. Don't panic if you find conflicting instructions. My unorthodox dyeing style, for example, was designed to maximize my working studio space and to give me specific results. Another artist may approach dyeing differently. Many paths can lead to the same goal.

Do keep in mind that safety should always come first. Because I work and teach beginning-level students in a historic (translates "old") building, I have avoided toxic processes whenever I can. There are other ways of dyeing, discharging, and painting, but I generally stick to what I know will work, while maintaining high safety standards. When you do use hazardous products, take the necessary precautions to protect yourself. Invest in a good respirator, wear gloves, use adequate ventilation, and know your materials. Dispose of them properly. Refer to the "Safety Precautions" for each process. Value yourself in this process of creation; your artwork will reflect that value.

I also try to think conservatively when I consider the environment, and you should too. Don't wear throw-away gloves if you can wear longer-lasting ones. Wash and reuse plastic sheeting, paint containers, and spray bottles. Recycle household containers and consider getting used buckets and storage bins from restaurants—they are usually happy to give them away. Just be sure to clearly label containers with their contents and keep them out of reach of children and pets.

A notebook is the perfect accompaniment to this book. I suggest you read through *Complex Cloth* to get an overview before actually beginning the processes. When you read a map, it always helps to know where you are going!

Work through the processes and make samples. Consider making samples of each process on different fabrics: silk, cotton, and rayon, for example. Use my ideas, and if others spin off from those, make samples of them too. Use a gluestick to mount samples in your notebook and write down your process, ideas, or other pertinent information as you go. You will be creating an invaluable resource.

Once your samples are complete, you are ready for "Studies and Explorations" (pages 151–54). Use this as a springboard. The guidelines are meant to shape your experience—to structure your work while you begin to make personal decisions about design, color, and fabric. The projects are designed to help you gain confidence. Once you have some experience, feel free to alter my projects. This is an indication that you've "gotten" it.

If I stood next to you and gave you any more advice, it would be this: Be fearless! If it makes sense, try it! No matter what happens, you will learn, and the next piece will only be stronger.

If you don't love it, don't do it. Life is too short to torture yourself with processes or projects you don't like.

Get busy!

Read through each process to make sure you have everything you need before starting. This is like cooking: never start a recipe until you know you have all the ingredients.

Organizing Your Work Space

The perfect work space is huge, well lit, and has not only hot and cold running water, but at least a hundred continuous feet of table space. "Ha!" you say? Don't worry. I don't have that kind of work space either.

The reality is our work space often must do double-duty. Don't worry if your work space is also the kitchen, laundry room, or living room—you are not alone. Few of us ever actually achieve that "room of one's own" to which Virginia Wolfe alluded. And even when we do, we struggle to fit in the wet stuff—dye buckets, paints, etc.— with the dry stuff—sewing machine, cutting table, and, in my case, the nine-year-old's desk.

The most basic components of a workable space are easy cleanup and good ventilation. As long as you can set up a fan and open a window, you can function adequately. It would be even better to have a garage or outdoor patio you could use for bleaching or dyeing during good weather. It is intimidating to work when you're afraid of spilling something on the carpet. If you must work in a high-maintenance area, buy a roll of plastic sheeting. You can cover everything and work with peace of mind.

If you can alter or design your space, consider the following. (If you don't have that much freedom, adapt as much as you can.)

❖ A sheet vinyl or concrete floor cleans up easily. If you work over carpet, roll out plastic sheeting. You can purchase sheet vinyl/linoleum at a building-supply store. Unroll this over flooring you want to protect.

❖ A convenient source of running water makes paint mixing and cleanup easier.

❖ A washer and dryer are invaluable. Nothing in this book will harm them, and you will still be able to use them for everyday washing and drying.

❖ Lighting is important. Extension lamps—the adjustable kind—are good. Sometimes you can find old-fashioned pull-down lamps from the 1950s at thrift stores. These are great.

❖ Storage and safety are critical. Label and date containers. Place solvents out of children's reach. Store paintbrushes in the bristle-up position. Keep your wet things— chemicals, dyes, and paints—separate from your dry things—sewing machine, cutting table, and fabric.

❖ A padded table and a hard surface are desirable. It is easy to construct a padded work table. Buy a 4' x 8' piece of plywood and a 4' x 8' or larger piece of ½"-thick foam rubber. Cut the foam to fit one side of the plywood. Wrap quilt batting and muslin around the foam-covered plywood. Staple the muslin and batting to the underside of the board, pulling them tight and smoothing as you staple. You can position this permanently on top of a table or lean it up against a wall when you don't need it. Cover with plastic sheeting to make it waterproof.

It is nice to have an additional work table, one that is not padded, but the kitchen table will do in a pinch. To adjust the height of your work table, add a concrete block under each leg.

❖ Keep your ironing board and iron at hand. If most of what you need is set up and ready to go, you'll want to work, and it will be easier to get started.

❖ A design wall is a must. Viewing your work on a design wall helps you evaluate what you have done while you are deciding what to do next. A sheet of foam core (available at art-supply stores) or foam board (available at building-supply stores) is lightweight, easily moved, and can be used again and again. Use T-pins to attach your work.

You can also glue clothespins to a piece of molding and hang the molding on the wall. Pin up your fabric for a quick look at your progress.

Ideally, your space should be one you don't have to clean up every time you stop working. If that isn't possible, don't let it stop you. Consider rolling storage carts, which make it easier to move everything into the closet or a spare room.

Red Square *by Jane Dunnewold, 1995, San Antonio, Texas, 45" x 85".*
Hand-painted and silk-screened cotton.

Where to Find Supplies

Sometimes finding supplies for a project is like a treasure hunt—materials turn up in unexpected places. Invariably, there will be a time when looking for just-the-right fabric, paint, or glue will prove to be a headache. The more familiar you are with suppliers, and the more adventurous you are when you shop, the easier it will be to find that perfect item when you need it.

There are many mail-order suppliers for the materials in this book. I like to support mail-order suppliers. They have built businesses based on reliability and professionalism, they provide vast quantities of supplies to those of us who love to work in textiles, and they know their products and stand behind them. Sometimes, mail order is the only way to get what you need. Often, the prices are better. Refer to "Resources" on page 156 when you begin to think about supplies. Many of these companies provide free catalogs, and many of the catalogs include design ideas as well as product information.

A neighborhood craft store offers a "browse" factor not possible with mail order. You have an opportunity to read packaging and study products you haven't used before. Regular sales and newspaper coupons are also an advantage of local shopping. Getting to know your craft retailer has other benefits. He or she may special-order products the store does not usually carry and may keep an eye out for you when new products are introduced.

Balance your sources. Shop at local craft and art stores, building-supply stores, and hardware stores. Be on the lookout for new ideas, materials, and products when you travel. Attend trade and specialty shows. The broader your knowledge of suppliers and products, the less time you'll spend on wild-goose chases.

Fabrics

The fabric you choose for creating complex cloth has a great deal to do with the success or failure of your project. The fabrics carried by your local fabric store have been treated with sizing—chemicals applied to the cloth to improve the way it looks and feels while still on the bolt. These chemicals can inhibit the fabric's ability to accept dyes, paints, and resists. Therefore, it is important to remove them before you begin work. Prewash every length of yardage you use with hot water and mild detergent. This is referred to as "scouring." Most dye suppliers carry a specially formulated detergent, Synthrapol®, but any household detergent should work.

The Procion® dyes recommended in this book are designed for cellulose (plant) fibers such as rayon, cotton, linen, and wood. Rayons and silks dye beautifully. Most cottons also accept dye nicely, but occasionally cotton fabric will be treated with chemicals you just can't remove. Choose another fabric and save that one for another process.

If the project you have chosen includes discharging—removing color with bleach—keep in mind that synthetic fibers will not be affected by bleach. Silk and wool are protein (animal) fibers and can be damaged by bleach. Cotton and rayon are the best fabrics for discharging.

The other processes discussed in these pages can be used on both natural and synthetic fibers. For more information on fiber content and fabric guidelines, refer to the chapter for each process.

The weave of the fabric can influence your results as much as the fiber content. A looser weave has a tendency to break up imagery—think of how a photograph might look if you held a window screen over it—and that makes it a poor choice for a detailed image. The tighter and smoother the weave, the more detail your image will have.

Don't forget mail-order suppliers when you need fabric. The resource section in the back of this book includes companies that offer very fine fabrics at good prices. An advantage of ordering through the mail is that many of the companies listed carry fabric prepared especially for dyeing and painting (referred to as "PFD"), which eliminates the need for prewashing and increases the likelihood that you will get great results. Mail-order suppliers also offer a wider variety of fabrics than you may be able to find locally. For example, 100% rayon fabric may be difficult to find in your local fabric store, but mail-order suppliers offer a wide range of colors and weaves.

While many techniques look great on colored backgrounds, choosing white or off-white fabric extends your range of possibilities, especially if you intend to dye the fabric. Some processes are transparent, and the background color influences how they look when complete. To get a feel for transparency and opacity in any one technique, make samples on both white and colored fabric. Make notes on the differences and plan accordingly when you begin larger projects.

Testing Fiber Content

One word of caution: It is not unusual to find fabric labeled 100% of a certain fiber when it is not. Misnaming is common in the fabric industry. I have found fabric labeled "100% acetate rayon" on more than one occasion. It is impossible for a fabric to be 100% acetate and 100% rayon. I believe inaccurate labeling has occurred because those of us who buy fabric have not protested. Polyester with the drape and feel of silk is still polyester, and the industry should be encouraged to find something other than a silklike term to call it.

In the meantime, carry a test kit with a small vial of bleach and a pack of matches in the car. I've never encountered a fabric store unwilling to give me a small sample of fabric. Take it out to the car and dip a corner in the bleach. If it discharges, you'll know it is a natural fiber.

Use a match to test the fiber content. If it burns to an easily crushed ash with the odor of burning hair, it is a natural fiber. If it burns to a hard bead not easily crushed, it is a synthetic, undyeable, unbleach-able fiber. If it doesn't burn to ash, don't despair! There are plenty of processes that work wonderfully on polyester and acetate blends.

Knowing fiber content levels the playing field and limits wasted time and materials. It helps you get great results fast!

Color

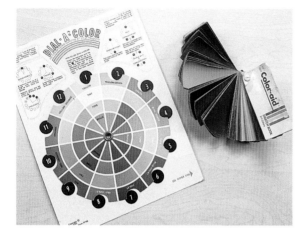

Color is one of those subjects capable of terrorizing many of us. I believe we all have an innate color sense if we will only trust it. Scientists and color theorists have simplified things for us with the color wheel, an invaluable tool. If you familiarize yourself with basic color terminology and use your color wheel until your own innate ability kicks in, you will make few mistakes.

Consider those mistakes you do make a learning experience. A great deal can be gained from looking at a length of cloth that didn't work in terms of color. Compare it to a length you like and note the differences. Pull out your color wheel and evaluate what you did as it relates to color theory.

Much of the success or failure of your work will be subjective. Many of the pieces my students dislike the most sell immediately when offered to the outside world.

Glossary of Color Terms

Hue: *Interchangeable term for color. Hue is the quality by which we distinguish colors from one another. There is no information provided by this term to indicate darkness, lightness, strength, or weakness.*

Primary colors: *The three colors or hues from which all other colors are made—red, blue, and yellow.*

Secondary colors: *The colors created when you mix two primary colors. When you mix blue and yellow, you get green. When you mix red and yellow, you get orange. When you mix red and blue, you get violet or purple. Green, orange, and violet are secondary colors.*

Tertiary colors: *The colors created when you mix two secondary colors or one primary and one secondary.*

Color wheel: *A visual tool for organizing the colors of the spectrum (red, orange, yellow, green, blue, and violet). In a circular format, the relationships between the colors are easier to visualize. A color wheel may be very simple—containing only the colors already mentioned—or it may be complex—containing primary, secondary, and tertiary colors and indicating relationships between colors.*

Warm colors: *Red, orange, yellow, and their tints and shades are warm colors. These hues feel warmer than their cool counterparts and remind us of warm things, such as fire and sunshine.*

Cool colors: *Blue, green, violet, and their tints and shades are cool colors. These hues feel cool and remind us of cool things, such as water, ice, and a shady retreat.*

Complementary colors: *Hues that are opposite each other on the color wheel. When complementary colors are mixed as beams of light, they make white light. When complementary colors are mixed as pigment, they create a muddy or brown color.*

Adjacent colors: *Hues that are next to each other on the color wheel. On the most basic color wheel, red is adjacent to orange and violet. On a more complex color wheel, red is adjacent to red-orange and red-violet.*

Achromatic colors: *White, black, or a mix of the two. An infinite number of grays may be mixed using white and black.*

At first, you may want to stick to a monochromatic color scheme. You can hardly go wrong following this approach. When you have worked with one color long enough to master the concepts of tint, tone, and shade, choose a more adventurous scheme. Try an analogous scheme—using secondary colors that are next to each other on the color wheel—or a complementary scheme—using different amounts of opposite colors creates a lively mix.

It helps to understand that one of your eye's natural responses to color is optical mixing (known as the "Bezold Effect"). Your eye perceives two colors simultaneously, so they merge into one new color. Use paint or crayons to make a red-and-green checkerboard with ½" squares. Mount your checkerboard on the wall. If you stand back and squint, the red and green will begin to mix. The farther you stand from your checkerboard, the more the colors mix, until you see neither red nor green, but a muddy sort of brown.

Tint: *A color with white added to it. Red mixed with white gives us a tint: pink.*

Shade: *A color with black added to it. Red mixed with black gives us a shade: maroon.*

Tone: *A color with gray added to it. Gray is, of course, a mixture of white and black, neither of which is truly a color. The shade of gray you choose to mix with red will determine the tone.*

Value: *The lightness or darkness of a color.*

Intensity or saturation: *The purity or strength of a color. A saturated color is pure and very intense. It does not contain any black or white.*

Monochromatic color scheme: *The use of one color and its tints, shades, and tones.*

Complementary color scheme: *The use of two colors opposing each other on the color wheel. It can also include tints, tones, and shades.*

Analogous color scheme: *The use of adjacent colors on the color wheel. It can also include tints, tones, and shades.*

Try another experiment to learn more about your eye's response to color. Paint or crayon an intense red, blue, or orange square on a white background. Stare at the square for one minute. At the end of the minute, switch your gaze to a blank sheet of white paper. You will see the color's opposite, or complement. Your eye always seeks the opposite of whatever hue it is viewing. Knowing this may not influence your color choices very much, but it will help you understand what is happening when you look at a color scheme.

Follow these color guidelines if you are still feeling shaky:

❖ Equal amounts of two complementary colors may turn into visual mud. In a complementary color scheme, choose one color as dominant and use its complement as a highlight.

This approach also works well when you are using more than two colors, such as in an adjacent or analogous color scheme. Using equal thirds of each hue may work, but it won't be as interesting as a less-balanced visual mix.

❖ A small dose of a complement adds punch to a design. If you are working with a complementary color scheme, such as orange and blue, you may use tints and shades of orange for the majority of your design with a small bright-blue element. The blue vibrates against the orange background and adds visual excitement. In an analogous color scheme, choose two of the colors as dominant and use the third as an accent. For example, use red-orange and orange as the dominant colors and yellow-orange as an accent. If you pull in a tiny blue-violet element, the design will really sing!

❖ Sometimes intensity can add visual excitement. If you are working on a monochromatic color scheme, consider using tints and shades as your background and a pure, saturated color as an accent.

❖ Value can enliven your color scheme in the same way. If the background of your fabric is a very pale or light value, a dark accent may seem to float on the surface. On a very dense, dark background, a pale image can also appear to float and might be just the accent that brings the fabric to life. Do not discount your ability to create the illusion of depth strictly through the knowledge and application of color theory. Imagery can float or recede based on how it relates to the background.

The colors you choose will be influenced by the textures, surfaces, and mediums you use as you apply them. Some paints have a shiny finish; others have a matte finish. The method of application you choose may give you dense or transparent coverage. Foils add shiny elegance. Puff paints add depth and texture. Do not be intimidated by your materials! And do not be afraid to experiment. There are no rules—only guidelines.

Japanese Raincoat (left) by Renita Kuhn and Jane Dunnewold, 1994, San Antonio, Texas. Dyed and overdyed cotton and silk. Silk-screened, foiled, and embellished with vintage and handmade beads.

Untitled Short Kimono (below) by Joanne Tschoepe, 1994, New Braunfels, Texas. Dyed and silk-screened cotton panels collaged with obi fabrics, then beaded.

Applications

There are lots of creative ways to apply dye, paint, bleach, or resist to fabric. You can cut a rubber stamp or stencil, make a silk screen, or apply your medium with a syringe, foam brush, or kitchen utensil. Your repertoire of application tools and techniques is limited only by your imagination. Every technique differs in terms of its look and how it affects the hand or feel of the finished cloth. Stamping makes the lightest impression. Stenciling gives you more control over how much medium you apply to the fabric. Silk screening provides consistent, total coverage. Choose the application technique based on the look you want: lighter, denser, looser, freer. You may want to make samples of each technique and use these as guides for later projects.

Stamping Basics

Of all the ways to apply dye, bleach, paint, or resist to fabric, stamping is the most immediate and accessible. Most of us had a chance to play with stamping when we were in grade school. Remember the potato prints of squares, triangles, and circles? My daughter came home from school once with a picture she had created by stamping painted halves of a green pepper!

You could carve a stamp from a potato as your first project, but it would last only a few days and would deteriorate as you used it. Instead, buy some erasers. Two kinds of erasers work best for stamping. The first is a gum eraser—light brown and very easy to cut with an X-Acto™ knife. The second is white plastic and is usually available at an office- or art-supply store. Do not buy pink or green rubber erasers with sloped ends. They are very dense and difficult to cut.

After you have carved several erasers, try working on a larger surface. Speedball® makes a print block that is bigger than a standard eraser but just as easy to cut. Monument Supply Companies manufactures a product called "sand-blasting stencil." It can be cut with either scissors or a knife and has the added advantage of a sticky backing. You can stick it to Plexiglas, providing a firm base and making the stamp easier to handle. Or try Fun Foam™, which is available in sheets, shapes, and blocks at craft stores. It can be cut into shapes with scissors or a knife and glued to Plexiglas with a hot-glue gun.

Everyday objects, such as bottle caps and keys, make wonderful stamps. Even foam food trays can be made into stamps. Cut pieces of foam and use a hot-glue gun to attach them to a backing, or use a sharp pencil to incise a pattern into the surface of the tray.

Do not overlook commercial stamps. Rubber stamps created for paper printing may work on a fabric surface if the detail is not too fine and the paint is not too thick. Block printing stamps—imported from Asia and often used in batik—offer classic designs and print bleach and paint beautifully.

Stamping Materials

Any or all of the following make good stamping materials. It's nice to have a collection of different materials to choose from when you want to make stamps.

Cutting surface: Used to protect your tabletop when carving a stamp. A self-healing mat is nice, but a heavy piece of cardboard is adequate.

E6000® adhesive: A thick, clear adhesive perfect for attaching stamps to Plexiglas. It can also be used to repair stamps. Do not use it with foam, as it will disintegrate the foam.

Erasers: Material used for carving a stamp. Use gum and white-plastic erasers. Gum erasers break down with use; white plastic has more staying power.

Fun Foam: Available in a variety of shapes and blocks as well as in larger sheets. Fun Foam is easy to carve, and the sheets can be glued to Plexiglas.

Plexiglas: A backing for stamps. Plexiglas is far superior to wood or cardboard because it allows you to see your printing as you work. Plexiglas blocks may be available as scrap at a plastic-supply store. Blocks that are at least ½" thick are perfect as backs for sand-blasting stencils or grouped erasers. Thinner Plexiglas will work, but it hurts your hand when you are printing.

Sand-blasting stencil: Material that comes in 12" x 30' rolls. It has a sticky backing that makes it is easy to apply to Plexiglas. Because sand-blasting stencil is thin, use two or more layers to give depth to the carved surface.

Speedball print blocks: Large, white plastic blocks that are easy to carve.

X-Acto knife: A knife for carving stencils. Choose a long, thin blade for more accurate cutting. A good knife, scaled to the job at hand, is invaluable. Do not substitute a heavier craft knife, and shy away from other blades. They are not as efficient as a thin blade.

You may also want: craft scissors; a hot-glue gun and gluesticks; assorted sizes and widths of foam brushes; foam food trays; found objects such as keys, corks, and bottle caps; and commercial stamps and a commercial stamp pad.

Salmon Duster by Jane Dunnewold, 1989,
San Antonio, Texas. Stamped cotton broadcloth.

Creating and Using Stamps

Understanding the process and choosing the right materials helps guarantee successful results. When you are stamping—whether you have chosen erasers, sand-blasting stencil, or incised foam—you are applying a pattern by pressing your stamp down firmly against the fabric. Whatever you are applying—dye, bleach, paint, resist—gets pushed against the fabric and, if too much has been applied, squishes up and around the edges of the stamp.

When you apply dye, bleach, paint, or resist, be conservative. Too much of any medium will blur your image. It doesn't take much to print evenly and consistently. Using a foam brush is preferable to dipping your stamp into a tray of bleach or paint. Dipping gives you far less control than applying the medium with a brush. A drippy stamp will never print a clear image. Use a foam brush instead of a bristle brush. A foam brush won't leave bristle marks on the finished cloth or be damaged by bleach. Also, foam brushes are inexpensive and available in a range of widths.

Fabric choice will vary, based on the results you have in mind. In general, a smoothly woven, lightweight fabric will produce the clearest imagery. The heavier the weave, the more a stamped image will be fractured. The detail of the stamp is lost if it doesn't register completely as you print it. If you would like to print on a rough-textured fabric, use a large-patterned, batik-type stamp, or cut a stamp from sand-blasting stencil or a printing block and eliminate the fine detail. Make sure your fabric is prewashed, dried, and ironed prior to stamping.

Stamping will go more smoothly if you have a soft surface to press against. If you do not have space for a padded table (see page 11), pad your work table with old towels or folded muslin.

Be diligent about cleanup. Most paints are harder to get off dry than wet! Use an old toothbrush and warm water to scrub away all paint residue. Your stamps will last a long time if you take care of them.

Scale is an important part of all the processes in this book. If you are coating a small eraser with paint, use a small foam brush. If you are using a larger print block, switch to a larger foam brush. Scale your tools to the size of your design.

...For Inspiration.....................................

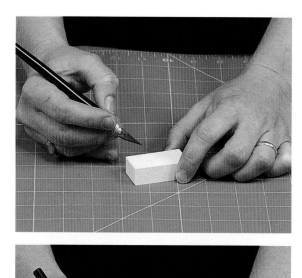

Carving a Stamp from an Eraser

Materials

Self-healing cutting mat or
  thick sheet of cardboard
Pencil or ball-point pen
White-plastic or gum eraser

X-Acto knife
E6000 adhesive
Straight pins

Optional Materials

Ink pad
Plexiglas

Heavy book

Procedure

Always work on a flat surface. Use a cutting mat or piece of cardboard to protect the table. Do not hold the stamp in your hand as you cut.

1. If desired, use a pencil or ball-point pen to draw a design on the eraser before cutting. It also is easy to cut spontaneously.
2. Using the X-Acto knife, make the first cut straight up and down. Cut into the eraser at least ¼". The deeper the cut, the better. Not cutting deep enough leaves areas of the stamp that will fill with paint as you print, blurring the final image.
3. Make the second cut at an angle to the first cut. Picture a wall in your mind. The first cut is the wall—your second cut should meet that wall without passing through it. This will preserve a firm base for the pieces of the eraser that remain. If you cut through them slightly every time you cut, the stamp will break easily.

    Cut curves with the same image in mind. Your first cut should be straight up and down. Use the point of the knife to make the curved cut. Your second cut will lean into that wall. Cut up to it, but don't cut through it.

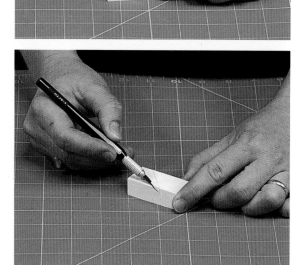

4. Use the tip of the blade to cut dots or squares within the surface of the eraser. Remember that it doesn't matter what the eraser looks like below the printing surface. You can dig out excess eraser any way that works for you, as long as the printing surface remains intact.

5. Erasers are very forgiving. If you accidentally cut out a piece you wanted to keep, use E6000 adhesive to glue it back. Use a straight pin to hold the piece in place while the glue dries.

Use an ink pad to check your image as you work. You can see where you might add another line or doodle.

Glue two or more erasers to a piece of Plexiglas to create a larger stamp. Choose a piece of Plexiglas about the same size as the stamps you want to glue together. Use E6000 to glue the erasers to the Plexiglas. Put a heavy book on top of the stamp while it is drying. (Sometimes the erasers shift slightly while drying. Weighting them prevents shifting.)

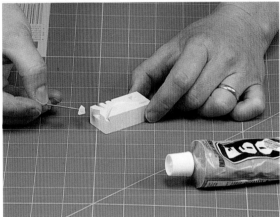

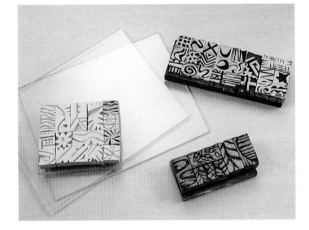

Cutting a Stamp from Foam or Sand-Blasting Stencil

Materials

Cutting mat or cardboard
Plexiglas
Foam or sand-blasting stencil
   (Foam is more difficult to cut than
   stencil material. Make sure the
   blade of your knife is very sharp.)

Hot-glue gun and gluesticks
Pencil or ball-point pen
X-Acto knife

Procedure

Always work on a flat surface. Use a cutting mat or piece of cardboard to protect the table. Do not hold the stamp in your hand as you cut.

1. Choose a piece of Plexiglas the size of the stamp you wish to make.
2. Cut a piece of foam or at least 2 pieces of sand-blasting stencil to fit the Plexiglas. If you are using foam, glue it to the Plexiglas with a hot-glue gun. If you are using sand-blasting stencil, peel off the backing paper and stick the stencil material to the Plexiglas. Apply 2 or more layers so you have an easier surface to cut. Wait 24 hours for the glue to bond permanently. (Otherwise the sand-blasting stencil may come off when you wash it the first time.)
3. If desired, use a pencil or ball-point pen to draw a design on the foam or sand-blasting stencil before cutting.
4. Using the X-Acto knife, make the first cut straight up and down. Cut into the foam or layers of sand-blasting stencil at least ¼". The deeper the cut, the better. Not cutting deep enough leaves areas of the stamp that will fill with paint as you print, blurring the final image.
5. Make the second cut at an angle to the first cut. Picture a wall in your mind. The first cut is the wall; your second cut should meet that wall without passing through it.

   Cut curves with the same image in mind. Your first cut should be straight up and down. Use the point of the knife to make the curved cut. Your second cut will lean into that wall. Cut up to it but not through it. Use the tip of the knife to remove tiny pieces.

Tips and Variations for Making Stamps

❖ If you want to carve readable letters, remember that they must be cut in reverse.

❖ Use E6000 to glue found objects to a piece of Plexiglas. Try precut foam shapes, lengths of string, two or more layers of felt cut into shapes, keys—the possibilities are limitless.

❖ Use a sharp pencil to incise a foam food tray. By pushing firmly against the foam, you can create an impression with a great deal of detail. Coat the tray lightly with paint to print. (Use a large foam brush.)

❖ Make a plain printing block, without cuts or patterning of any kind. Coat the block with paint and use a cotton swab, a blunt pencil, or an eraser to draw on the painted surface, removing paint as you work. Print this one-of-a-kind image, paint the block again, and continue.

Stenciling Basics

Stenciling is a relatively simple method of applying images to fabric. A stencil makes it possible to repeat an image many times using different processes while maintaining the size and basic design of your image.

Commercial stencils are available at art- and craft-supply stores. They are plastic and very durable. Unfortunately, you cannot alter size, and you may not find a particular image you are seeking. Learning to cut your own stencils is easy and will broaden your design repertoire.

You can cut stencils from thin sheets of plastic, like that used to make quilting templates, or from cover-weight paper, such as a file folder or a similar weight of cardboard. Plastic sheets are available at craft stores. A file folder or similar-weight cardboard is easy to cut and, when properly prepared, lasts as long as plastic.

Inspiration for stencils comes from many sources. When you are thinking of translating an idea into a stencil, sketch it first, or use the photocopier to make an image you can study. Part of the appeal of stenciling is how it simplifies complicated shapes and its emphasis on positive and negative contrast in a design. The positive part of your design is the design itself—a hand-drawn image, for example. The negative part of the design is the area around the drawing. We usually think of the negative area as empty space, but when you are working with design, it is important to recognize that the empty space also has a shape. If the shape is interesting, it will make your overall design stronger. Learning to recognize or "see" positive and negative space strengthens your ability to create complex cloth.

Keep the concept of positive and negative space in mind as you plan your stencil. If you design a stencil with lots of detail in the center, then proceed to cut out the center shape, you will lose all the carefully planned detail. Instead, think in terms of individual elements. For example, if you are cutting a branch with leaves, cut the branch as a long, single element. Cut each leaf individually and separate it slightly from the branch. Add berries by cutting small individual berries rather than by cutting out a cluster of berries. If you want to add a bird, think about how to represent the bird in several connected units. The body might be separate from the wings. A crest might be separated just a bit from the top of the head. The best way to learn how to plan a stencil is to draft a pattern, then cut a stencil.

Creating and Using Stencils

There are many tools for applying dye, bleach, paint, or resist to a stencil: stencil brushes, bristle brushes, foam brushes, sea sponges, and synthetic sponges all work well. Stencil brushes are designed so the bristles are cut straight across the bottom. This provides a flat surface that is perfect for applying paint to the open areas of the stencil. (Do not use natural-bristle brushes with bleach; the bristles will disintegrate.) Foam brushes, sea sponges, or synthetic sponges are all great choices for use with stencils. Each has a distinctive texture. Each also can provide total coverage if desired. Remember to scale the size of your brush or sponge to the size of the stencil.

You can use a wide range of fabrics for stenciling. Avoid bleach if you are using silk, but feel free to try rayon, cotton, and silk with any of the other mediums. Heavier fabrics—even fabrics with a pile, like cotton velvet and rayon velveteen—can be stenciled.

Storing stencils properly contributes to their longevity. Store smaller stencils in marked file folders. Keep similar imagery together and label the folders for easy access. Store them in an upright position to keep the stencils from warping. You can also punch a hole in the corner of stencils and hang them from a cup hook in your studio or workroom.

. . . For inspiration . . . .

Crop Kimono by Sarah Kalvin and Agnes Welsh Eyster, 1995, San Antonio, Texas. Dyed and silk-screened cotton. (Original pattern by Sarah Kalvin)

Cutting a Stencil

Materials

Cutting mat or cardboard
Cardboard file folder
    or template plastic
Pencil or ball-point pen
X-Acto knife

Duct tape or packing tape
Clear polyurethane or acrylic
    spray sealer
Newspaper, plastic sheeting,
    or a plastic garbage bag

Optional Materials

Spray adhesive
Stencil-burning tool

Carbon paper

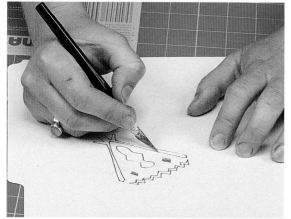

Procedure

Always work on a flat surface. Use a cutting mat or piece of cardboard to protect the table. Do not hold the stencil in your hand as you cut.

1. Choose the design you will translate into a stencil. Draw a design yourself, or photocopy or alter an image from another source. (See "Tips and Variations for Making Stencils" on page 31.)

2. Transfer the design to the cardboard file folder or template plastic. There are three ways to do this: draw the design freehand, coat the back of the design with spray adhesive and apply it to the file folder or template plastic, or use carbon paper to trace the design.

3. Use an X-Acto knife to cut out the design. It may help to hold the knife still and move the stencil material when you are cutting curves. If you are cutting a large stencil, it may be easier to stand up while working.

    If you are using template plastic, use a sharp knife or a stencil-burning tool to cut out the shapes. Many people like to use a burning tool. When you plug it in, the tip heats up and melts the plastic instead of cutting it. I prefer an X-Acto knife and file folder.

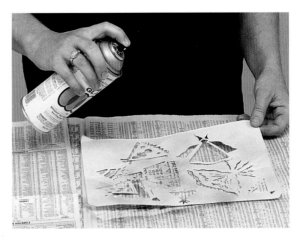

4. If there are thin "bridges" on the stencil, you may want to reinforce them with duct tape or packing tape. Use slivers of tape to strengthen thinner sections of your design and to repair mistakes or tears.

5. Once you have cut a stencil from a file folder, it is important to seal it with a clear polyurethane or acrylic spray. Sealing the cardboard stencil protects it from dampness in both the application and cleaning processes. Lay the stencil down on newspaper, plastic sheeting, or a plastic garbage bag. Spray the front of the stencil until it is saturated. Allow the spray to dry, turn the stencil over, and spray the back. When the stencil has dried completely, front and back, spray it again. Once the stencil dries the second time, it will be impervious to water.

6. When the stencil is dry, it is ready to use.

Always clean stencils immediately after use with cool water and a soft sponge. Lay the stencil flat in the sink and sponge away excess dye, bleach, paint, or resist. Hang the stencil to dry from a clothesline or clothespin it to a hanger and let it drip-dry over the sink.

Store stencils in an upright position, away from direct sunlight and dust.

Tips and Variations for Making Stencils

❖ Use a photocopy machine to make several stencils of the same design in different sizes.

❖ Look for Dover Publications' design books in your library or bookstore. (See the "Bibliography" on page 155.) The illustrations in these books are in the public domain, which means there is no copyright on the material included in them. The books are very inexpensive. Dover also publishes a series of "cut-your-own" stencils.

Silk-Screening Basics

Silk screening can be simple as described here, or it can involve large, complicated screens and equipment. This section will teach you how to produce a screen capable of enhancing a fabric surface with limited patterning. Your design will not function as a true repeat in the sense that some designs match side by side and repeat regularly. (See the books listed in the "Bibliography" on page 155 for more information on designing repeats.) Instead, the design created here should be thought of as a "single-unit" screen—a single pattern that can be used as a scattered overall design or as an overlapping design in one or more colors.

The invention of the silk screen revolutionized the printing world. Suddenly, it became easier to makes lots of copies of an image and to make them fast! Originally, real silk was used as the mesh on a silk screen. Today, most silk screens use a polyester mesh.

Within the field of silk screening, there are a number of possible ways of preparing a screen and making a print. Some of these techniques are tedious and can make it impossible to "reclaim" (clean for reuse) the screen.

The applications in this book are based on photo emulsion. This is a light-sensitive chemical developed specifically for use with silk screens. To make the photo emulsion, you mix silk-screen emulsion and sensitizer, a light-sensitive material that allows an image to be developed on the mesh surface of the screen. The silk-screen emulsion is a water-based medium that acts as a binder, enabling the sensitizer to stick to the mesh surface.

The emulsion is applied to a screen and allowed to dry. A design is photocopied onto a transparency (acetate), then attached to the screen. The screen is exposed to a bright light. The areas of photo emulsion exposed to the light harden; the areas protected by the design on the transparency do not. After the exposure time has elapsed, the silk screen is sprayed with a high-pressure hose, and the parts of the design that didn't harden wash away.

It is possible to expose a silk screen coated with photo emulsion by using natural sunlight. However, this is an unpredictable process.

Untitled Long Vest *by Michelle Newman, 1995, San Antonio, Texas. Silk-screened velveteen.*

For Inspiration

The time of year and day can greatly influence your results. A light table is an invaluable tool. If you do not have access to or cannot afford a commercial light table, you can easily set up a light that will work. Consider constructing your own light source for more control over the exposure process. (See "Building a Light Source" on page 45.)

All kinds of designs are appropriate for use with silk screens. To begin, you may want to adapt an illustration from design books such as the Dover series. (See "Tips and Variations for Making Stencils" on page 31 and "Art and Copyright" on page 121.) Ink or black-marker drawings work beautifully. The most important factor is contrast. Black and white or positive/negative contrast is important. An image with large areas of gray—especially shaded areas that blend into one another—does not provide enough contrast to make a clear print. A color picture can be translated into a black-and-white image on a photocopier, but it doesn't usually have enough contrast to make a successful silk screen. Choose a dense, black image for your first screen. Once you have made a successful screen and understand the process, you can experiment with a broader selection of designs.

Once your silk screen is exposed, washed, and dried, it can be used with dyes, paints, and resists. *Photo emulsion cannot be used with household bleach.* The bleach will melt the photo emulsion. In general, thicker paints give better results than thinner paints. Avoid paints that contain glitter, since the glitter will not pass through the mesh and can clog the screen.

In silk-screened art prints, oil-based inks are the preferred medium. Working with fabric makes it possible to use water-based paints, many of which have been formulated especially for use on fabric. Several paint companies manufacture fabric paints specifically for silk screening, but any water-based fabric paint can be adapted to the silk-screening process. (See "Comparing Fabric Paints" on pages 158 –59.) Some paints change the "hand" of the fabric (the way it feels to the touch) less than others. You may prefer certain fabric paints over the paint sold specifically for screening. Some paints have a plastic appearance when screened onto cloth, while others have a matte finish.

The actual silk-screening process involves pulling the dye, paint, or resist across the surface of the screen with a squeegee. This action forces the medium through the open areas of the mesh and prints the design. The nature of the technique allows you to exercise a great deal of control over the amount of medium applied to the fabric. It also provides the best total coverage of any application technique. By adjusting for texture and weight, it is possible to print a thick, handwoven fabric as easily as a lightweight silk. I cannot overemphasize the importance of making samples. The broader your experience with different fabrics and processes, the more developed your complex cloth.

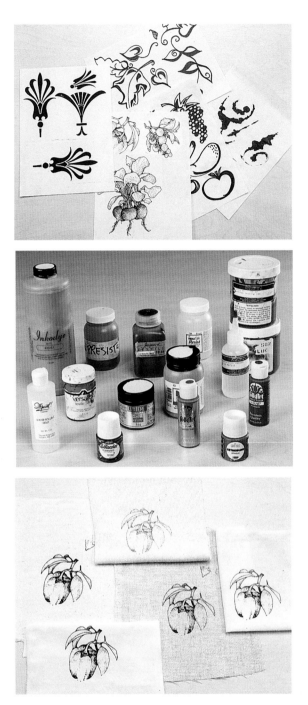

Marc's Piece *by Jane Dunnewold, 1991,*
San Antonio, Texas, 48" x 52". Dyed and overdyed
silk broadcloth. Silk-screened, foiled, beaded,
and embroidered.

Preparing a Silk Screen

Materials

White paper
Black marking pen
Transparency material (acetate)
Hardwood for the frame*,
  ready-made screen,
  or 4 artists' stretcher bars
Hammer or staple gun and staples
¼"-diameter cotton cording
Silk-screen mesh**
Screwdriver
Craft scissors
Duct tape
Stiff scrub brush
Household cleanser
Hose with power-spraying capability
A room that can be darkened
  during the drying time

4 blocks, ceramic tiles, or coffee
  cups to elevate the screen
  while the emulsion is drying
Electric fan
Speedball Silkscreen Emulsion***
Speedball Sensitizer***
Measuring spoons
Small dish and spoon for mixing
  photo emulsion
Squeegee to fit the screen
Light source
Sheet of glass to fit inside
  the silk-screen frame
Timer

Optional Materials

India ink or transparency marker   Rub-on lettering

*Determine the size of your frame by measuring the outside dimensions of your design. Add 2" to the length and width of the design. For example, if the design is 8" x 10", the frame would need to be 10" x 12". Silk-screen supply companies sell frame parts that are heavier than artists' stretcher bars. These will not easily warp.

**For best results, the silk-screen mesh should be at least 2" larger on all sides than the frame. Size 10xx or 12xx mesh is used for printing fabric. Choose a multifilament mesh instead of a monofilament mesh—it does a better job of holding the photo emulsion.

***If you choose another light-sensitive photo emulsion product, read the manufacturer's instructions carefully before beginning. Another company's emulsion may have different requirements than those described here.

Procedures

PREPARING THE DESIGN

Create your silk-screen design in one of the following ways:

1. Draw a design on white paper. Typing or copy-machine paper is a good choice for a small screen. If you are making a larger design, use drawing paper or tape several sheets of paper together. Use a very black marker to draw the design. The more contrast, the more successful the screen. Try to draw the design the right size for the screen. If necessary, use a copier to enlarge or reduce the design to fit the screen.

2. Use rub-on lettering to make a design, either freeform or legible wording. Put the lettering on white paper.

3. Transfer a design from a design book such as Dover. Choose a dense, black design for best results.

TRANSFERRING THE DESIGN

Transfer your design to a transparency in one of the following ways:

1. Take your original to a copy shop and have them print it onto a clear transparency. If you want to make a screen with more than one of the same image on it, order more than one transparency. Your image can also be enlarged or reduced at this point.
2. If you have access to a copier and purchase transparencies at an office-supply store, you can make the transparency yourself. Follow the transparency-manufacturer's instructions.
3. Use India ink or a marker specifically designed for transparencies to draw directly on the acetate. The ink must be opaque to block light during the exposure process. This as your original; copy if desired.

ASSEMBLING THE FRAME AND PREPARING THE SCREEN

The simplest way to prepare a screen is to purchase a ready-made screen from an art-supply store or a mail-order supplier. If you purchase a prestretched screen, tape and clean it, following steps 4–7 on page 39. Allow it to dry completely before coating it with photo emulsion. If you prefer to make a screen, follow the directions below.

1. Assemble the frame by inserting the notched ends into one another and hammering the joint gently until the ends are flush. If the frame is properly joined, the corners will be square and firm, and the frame will feel stable.
2. If you are using artists' stretcher bars, staple diagonally across the seam at each corner to strengthen the joint.

3. If your frame has grooves, you can attach the silk-screen mesh with cotton cording. Unroll a piece of cording slightly longer than the circumference of the frame. Lay the mesh on top of the frame, positioning it so the excess mesh is evenly distributed on each side. Starting at a corner, use the screwdriver to push the cording into the groove.

Working across the shortest edge first, push down 1" to 2" of cording, then pull on the alternate side of the mesh to keep it straight and squared. (The reason you cut the mesh larger than the frame was so you could use the edge of the frame for leverage while stretching the mesh. Use that leverage to your advantage now.)

When you reach the next corner, push the cording into the groove, around the corner, and down the next side. Work around the perimeter of the frame, alternately pushing down cording and pulling on the opposite side to keep the mesh squared. When you reach the beginning, trim any excess cording. Push the end down firmly into the groove. The screen should be very tight and smooth. If it isn't tight enough, pull up some of the cording and try again. When you are satisfied with the tension, use craft scissors to trim the mesh flush with the edge of the frame.

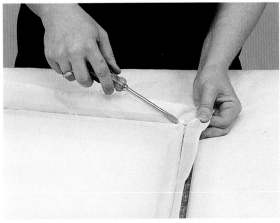

If you are stapling the mesh, begin in the middle of the shortest side. Lay the mesh on the frame so the excess mesh is evenly distributed on each side. Staple 2 or 3 staples at a slight angle, into the middle of the short side.

Pull the mesh taut and staple 2 or 3 staples at an angle into the middle of the frame's opposite side. Use the edge of the frame for leverage.

Always work on opposite sides at the same time and always staple on a slight angle. This helps keep the mesh taut and smooth as you work and allows for greater tension than you can achieve if you staple parallel to the frame's edge. If the staples don't go all the way into the frame, use a hammer to push them down.

Work all the way around the frame, alternating sides as you staple. Do the corners last. When you are finished stapling, use craft scissors to trim the mesh flush with the edge of the frame.

4. It is important to tape the silk screen when you have finished attaching the mesh to the frame. Taping protects the frame from moisture and prevents liquid from leaking through joints where the mesh meets the frame. Start on the back (the flat side) of the frame. Cut a piece of duct tape the length of one side. Apply the tape so it overlaps the mesh by at least 1". Make sure it is straight and smooth. Tape the other 3 sides in the same manner.

Next, tape the sides of the frame. The tape should overlap the first piece of tape you applied on each side, wrap around the edge and side of the frame, and reach partially onto the front. If your frame is very thick, it may take more than one piece of tape to cover each side. The important thing is to completely encase the frame in tape.

Turn the frame over to the front. Cut pieces of duct tape the same length as the inner dimensions of the frame. Apply them so they line up exactly with the tape on the back. The tape on the front and back should overlap onto the mesh exactly the same distance. The tape applied to the front should extend part way up the inside edge of the frame. Finish taping this inside edge. If wood shows anywhere on this inside edge, add more tape to seal it. Practice makes perfect!

5. Allow the tape to cure 24 hours before you use the screen; otherwise, it may loosen and wash off.

6. After the tape cures, scrub the screen thoroughly with cleanser and a stiff brush. Specialty cleansers are available from screen suppliers, but a household cleanser works just as well.

Scrubbing the mesh removes sizing, grease, and oil that could inhibit the emulsion's ability to adhere smoothly to the screen. Scrubbing also roughs up the mesh and gives the emulsion a better surface to stick to.

7. Allow the screen to dry thoroughly before applying the emulsion.

EXPOSING THE SILK SCREEN

When your silk screen is dry, you can coat it with photo emulsion and expose it to produce your design. Remember, the emulsion is light sensitive. You must work quickly. Prepare your drying room prior to coating the screen, because you won't be able to lay the coated screen down once the emulsion has been applied.

Always make sure you have enough time to apply the emulsion and expose the screen within a 24-hour period. Once the screen has been coated with emulsion, it can be kept in a dark room (or a plastic garbage bag) overnight, but if you wait too long it may not expose properly. It is better to coat the screen and expose it as soon as it dries.

1. Get the drying room ready. A screen cannot dry in a vertical position; it must be flat. Place 4 blocks of wood, ceramic tile, or coffee cups in front of the fan. These objects will support the screen while it dries. Lay the screen down and determine exactly where the supports should be placed (for each corner of the frame).

Make sure the room can be completely darkened. Turn off the lights.

2. Mix the sensitizer and emulsion using a 4:1 ratio. If you use a table-spoon measure, you will have enough emulsion to coat two 8½" x 11" screens. Mix only as much as you need. While you can keep premixed emulsion in the refrigerator for about a week, it is less reliable than a fresh mix.

3. Elevate one end of the screen and pour a thin stream of emulsion across the upper edge of the screen, where the mesh meets the tape. (This taped area is called the "well.")

4. Use the squeegee to pull the emulsion across the surface of the mesh. Always pull the squeegee toward you. Squeegee in an even motion from the upper edge of the mesh to the lower edge. Do not stop on the surface of the mesh — this can cause lines or holes in the emulsion.

Do not let the coated mesh touch the tabletop or counter. Anything that touches the emulsion will remove it from the mesh.

4. When you have squeegeed from top to bottom, turn the screen over and squeegee again on the back.

5. When the mesh is completely covered with an even coating of emulsion on both front and back, carry it into the darkened drying room. Carry it flat, back side down. Put its corners on the supports you arranged in advance.

    The back of the screen should always be down. If drips of emulsion form as the screen dries, it is better to have them on the back of the screen than on the front.

6. Leave the screen in front of the fan in the darkened room until the emulsion is completely dry (30 minutes to 1 hour). When you check the screen to see if it is dry, always touch the edge rather than the middle of the screen. If the screen isn't dry, your finger could pull off emulsion and leave a hole.

7. While the silk screen is drying, prepare to expose it. Set up a light source. (See "Building a Light Source" on page 45.) Put your transparency near the light source, along with a piece of glass cut to fit the screen and a timer. Use the piece of glass to weight the transparency, ensuring even contact with the screen.

8. When the emulsion is dry, bring the screen into the room where you will be exposing it. Lay the screen flat on the table, right side up. Position the transparency in the middle of the screen. Lay the glass on top of the transparency.

9. Position the surface of the screen at least 12" from the light. If the screen is too close to the light, it will not expose properly—the light will burn the center of the image so it is impossible to wash out. The screen may need to be farther than 12" from the light if it is a large screen. Follow these guidelines to determine distances from screen to light:

Screen Size	Distance from Light	Exposure Time (minutes)
8" x 10"	12"	12
10" x 14"	12"	12
12" x 18"	15"	16
16" x 20"	18"	20
18" x 24"	18"	22

    If the distance from your light source to your screen varies from those mentioned above, do at least one test exposure to determine the correct time or adjust your light-to-screen distance so it conforms to the guidelines listed above.

10. Turn on the light. Referring to the chart, set the timer for the appropriate time. Don't leave the room! Stay near the light so you can turn it off as soon as the timer rings. If the screen is overexposed—left under the light too long—the emulsion can get too hard to wash out.

11. When the timer rings, take the screen to your water source and spray it with a high-powered hose. Spray the entire surface of the mesh and continue to spray until the unexposed areas of the design begin to wash away. If the screen has been properly prepared and exposed, it will be possible to wash out even the smallest areas of detail.

12. Once the design has been washed out, the emulsion is very fragile. Allow the screen to dry for 24 hours before using it to print.

Store screens in an upright position when not in use, so they will not warp.

RECLAIMING THE SILK SCREEN

1. To change or redo the design on the screen, simply immerse it in 1" of household bleach for 10 minutes. If the screen won't fit in a pan or the sink, lay a towel saturated with bleach on the surface of the mesh. The emulsion will melt and/or loosen.

2. Using a stiff brush, scrub the screen. Rinse thoroughly; bleach residue on the screen or under the tape can cause problems.

3. When the screen is dry, coat and expose it again.

Troubleshooting

If large portions of your design wash away, the screen was not cleaned properly, the exposure time was not long enough, and/or the design on the transparency was not black enough. Reclaim the screen with bleach, rinse thoroughly, and try again.

If portions of the design will not wash away, the screen was overexposed and/or the details (very fine lines, for example) were not black enough to register. Reclaim the screen with bleach, rinse thoroughly, and try again.

Untitled #8 by Jane Dunnewold, 1993, San Antonio, Texas, 48" x 62". Dyed and overdyed silk noil slashed and backed with velvet. Silk-screened, foiled, and puff-painted.

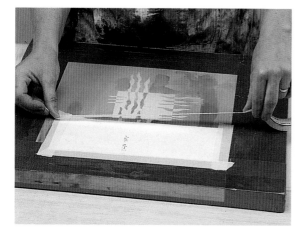

Tips and Variations for Making a Silk Screen

❖ To print a mirror image or right and left version of a design, you need two screens. Use the transparency to make the first screen, with your design facing right. Flip the transparency over so it is facing left for the second screen.

❖ To print segments of a design, tape off parts of the image. Use masking tape. (Do not use duct tape; removing it can damage the emulsion.) To block out larger areas of the design, tape paper or newsprint over them temporarily.

❖ Occasionally, a screen's emulsion will develop small holes after washing. This may happen along the taped edges if bleach was not thoroughly removed during the reclaiming process. Repair holes and breaks in the emulsion with duct tape. Put the tape on the back of the screen, or the squeegee will pull it off. Let the tape cure for 24 hours before using.

For Inspiration

Building a Light Source

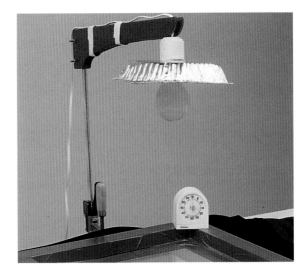

Materials

Tin snips
12" aluminum pie plate
300W BBA #1 photoflood bulb
 (available from a
 photography supplier)

Standard light socket
Newspaper, 2 yds. muslin, or
 old towel
Piece of black felt larger than
 the frame being exposed

Optional Materials

Duct tape

Picture-hanging wire

Procedure

1. Using tin snips, cut a hole in the center of an aluminum pie plate so you can place it over the light socket.
2. Screw in the light bulb.
3. Suspend the light at least 12" above the surface where you will expose the photo emulsion (see the chart on page 41). The light must shine directly onto the surface below. You must be able to control the distance between the light source and the silk screen. Tape or wire the cord and socket to a hanger so you can hang it from a table edge, build a stand from wood and wire or tape the light to the stand, or scavenge an old lamp stand from a thrift store or garage sale.

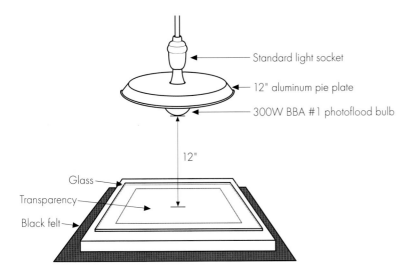

4. Using the newspaper, muslin, or towel, pad the area under the light. Cover it with the black felt. Center the screen under the light source.

Floating Blocks by Jane Dunnewold, 1996, San Antonio, Texas, 52" x 52". Cotton hand painted with dye and silk-screened. Interfacing hand painted with dye.

Processes

The processes described here are the basis of all the complex cloth you will create. A mature cook usually has a few basic recipes—tried-and-true favorites that can be altered, adjusted, and seasoned into a host of different dishes. You will use a similar approach to create complex cloth. Once you have mastered the processes and applications, you will be free to mix and match, adjust and season, to create yardage that is uniquely your own.

These processes are arranged in an easy-to-follow sequence. Since dyes are usually the first step in creating complex cloth, we begin with dyes and ways to apply them. The following processes—bleach, paints, resists, foils, and photocopying—are used to add depth to the dyed fabric. You will eventually develop your own sequences—ordering your processes to fit your desired complex cloth. In the meantime, remember to make samples and to label your samples so you can re-create them later.

. . . .

It is crucial that you read and understand the processes before you begin. Cultivating this work habit will save you time, money, and effort. Nothing is worse than starting a particular process, only to find halfway through that you're missing one of the most important components. Work smart; read everything first.

In some cases, there will be basic recipes to refer to in addition to the project instructions. Always read these in advance as well, as they help make the process and its steps clearer.

Dyes

My dyeing processes are different from those you may have read of or learned from other sources, and it is important that you understand why. When I first began dyeing, the class I taught was in a very small space and was very short. Traditionally, dyebaths are prepared by mixing salt, water, and dye, then adding soda ash. Near-constant stirring is part of the recommended process. We followed these instructions and got nice results. But I started experimenting on the side and found I could get striking results and a perfect pattern surface if I mixed the salt, soda ash, and water, then added the dye and fabric. While this is unorthodox, it works; the cloth I have created attests to that! If your desired result is evenly dyed cloth, do not follow these directions. Instead, check the variations I have listed on page 56. If you still need information, consult one of the sources listed in the "Bibliography" on page 155.

I also handle batching in an unorthodox way. (See "Glossary of Dyeing Terms and Products" on page 49.) Because the classes I taught met once a week, students were faced with the challenge of batching their wet fabrics in order to transport them home. This involved shortening the time the fabric was in the dye buckets. It also meant we had plastic bags and sheeting to clean up because we had to wrap all that fabric. I am troubled by abuse of the environment and throwing out plastic. We solved it by leaving the fabric in the dye solution—literally in the bucket—for the duration of the batching time. Students took turns coming in the next morning to wash out the fabric, and those who couldn't come in took their fabric home in the bucket after pouring off most of the excess dyebath.

Instead of wrapping your fabric when the immersion time has elapsed, leave everything in the bucket and wash it out twenty-four hours later. This is easier on you and on the world around you.

Fiber-Reactive Dyes

I prefer Procion MX fiber-reactive dyes, which are formulated for use on cellulose (plant) fibers such as rayon, cotton, linen, and wood. All the ideas and recipes included in this book use Procion MX dyes because they are easily cured and can be used in many ways.

A chemical change occurs in the dyebath that binds the dye molecules permanently to the fiber molecules, providing brilliant, colorfast results. The dye molecules chemically react with the fiber molecules in a process of electron sharing, which is a very strong chemical bond. This is very different from fabric paints, which do not bond with the fiber. Instead, fabric paints sit on the surface of the cloth, affecting the hand or feel of the fabric in a way Procion dyes do not.

Within the Procion family are several types of dye, including Procion MX, Procion H, and Sabracron® F. Each type has different requirements for its use. All the dyes are made by one manufacturer and sold to dyehouses, where they are packaged and sold under their own brand names. A good supplier will indicate what type of Procion dye you are buying, but if in doubt, ask when you order.

One ounce of dye will dye two pounds of fabric a medium value, which translates into six T-shirts or approximately nine square yards of fabric. There are a number of variables that will affect the outcome of your dyeing. These include:

❖   The type of fabric you choose and where it comes from. Rayons can be counted on to dye deep and dark, depending on the amount of dye you use. Cottons and silks also dye beautifully, but in my experience, they are more likely to have been treated with chemicals that interfere with the dye process and are difficult to remove. Some fabrics also have slubs, oils, gums, and other impurities that interfere with the dye process.

Ordering cloth from a mail-order supplier who stocks PFD or dye-ready fabrics can save time and

money. Having said that, I recommend browsing through your local fabric store. Much of their stock will dye satisfactorily, and experimenting with fabric from a variety of sources broadens your resource base. A piece of yardage that won't take the dye can usually be used for another series of techniques. *Synthetics, including blends with a synthetic, will not dye.* Remember, if you are in doubt as to fiber content, burn a swatch before you buy.

❖   Dyes provide pure, transparent color. If you dye white fabric, you will have a pure-hued fabric. If your cloth is off-white or another color, that color will affect the color of the fabric. Studying the section on color theory (pages 16–18) will help you predict what your final results will be.

❖   The amount and color of the dye you use will influence the results. Most recipes give dye amounts meant to dye a medium value. I have found that this is fairly subjective; you and I may not agree about what a medium value is. If you want dark values, you will need to use more dye.

Experiment with different amounts of dyes and record your results in a notebook so you can retrace your steps. Finding your own personal series of colors and values is more satisfying than using someone else's formulas. You must use more dye powder for some colors, such as turquoise and black, to get the same value or depth of color you would get with other colors, such as fuchsia or yellow. This is an inequity among each dye's components, and the best you can do is learn to compensate when you measure out the dye.

There are dyes formulated for different fabric types. If in doubt, ask

questions when you order the dyes. While you are learning, experiment with as many different dyes and fabrics as you can and make samples, samples, samples!

❖   Water hardness/softness affects the dyebath. If you have hard water—as I do in Texas—you may choose to add a water-softening product to your dyebath. If you do not add softener to hard water, the chemicals that make the water hard will work to push the dye molecules out of suspension, which can create very interesting effects but will never give you evenly dyed fabric.

The basic components of a dyebath are dye-stock solution (dye powder mixed with water), water, soda ash, and noniodized salt. Soda ash and salt facilitate the chemical change that occurs as the dye molecules bind themselves to the fibers. Depending on your choice of dye applications, you may also use urea, Calgon or Metaphos, Calsolene oil®, and PRO Thick.

Procion dyes can be mixed according to basic color theory for a wide variety of pure hues and shades. Dye powder can be stored in a cool place indefinitely with little loss of intensity. Dye-stock solutions can be stored for several weeks in the refrigerator. However, once soda ash has been added to the dye-stock solution, the dye begins to react and is "exhausted" in six to eight hours. It is important to mix only as much solution as you will need for your dye application.

Procion dyes must be set to make them color- and lightfast. Fabric can be steamed or batched, or a fixative can be applied.

Steaming requires the use of a steamer, which you can purchase from a dye supplier or construct at home using a home canner. Professional steamers are expensive, and the steaming process is cumbersome. You must roll the dry cloth in Pellon® and newsprint, then steam the roll for several hours. Steaming is usually the best setting method for hand-painted silk.

Batching refers to keeping dampened cloth warm and moist for twenty-four to forty-eight hours. Batching gives the dye molecules the environment and time they need to bond effectively with the fiber molecules. After the batching period has elapsed, you can rinse and wash the fabric or use it in another process.

You can also purchase chemical fixatives from a dye supplier. You apply the dye-stock solution, then wait for the fabric to dry. When it's dry, you paint the fixative onto the cloth, wait a predetermined length of time, then wash out the fixative. This is an easy way to set your dyes, but adds some expense.

Glossary of Dyeing Terms and Products

Batching: The process of keeping a newly dyed fabric damp and at room temperature for twenty-four to forty-eight hours. During this time, the chemical reaction begun in the dyebath is completed.

Calsolene oil: A wetting agent, which means it breaks the surface tension of the water and helps the water saturate the fabric so it can more easily absorb the dye.

Chemical water: A solution of urea and water that can be premixed to speed dye-preparation time. It can be stored several months in a cool place. A softener or a thickener may be added to it at the same time the dye is added.

Dye stock: A solution of dye and water. Chemicals can be added to the stock, depending on the technique you are using. It can be stored about a week in the refrigerator.

Fiber-reactive dyes: Synthetic dyes available to home dyers in several formulations, including Procion MX and Procion H. Packaged under different brand names, these dyes can be used with cellulose and some protein fibers. Fiber-reactive dyes chemically bond with the fiber molecules.

Immersion dyeing: Immersing fabric into a bucket or washing machine filled with water, dye, and chemicals.

Ludigol®: A trade name for a chemical used in painted applications of dye. It increases the dye's ability to set during the batching period. Also marketed as PRO Chem Flakes.

Metaphos: A chemical used with sodium alginate to make it flow more smoothly when a thickened dye application is desirable. Also a water softener.

Migration: Dye spreading or bleeding into areas where it is not wanted.

Overdyeing: Immersing fabric in a second dyebath, usually a different hue, to achieve variation and depth in the surface color.

PreVal® Sprayer: A refillable glass bottle with a compressed air canister on top. You fill the bottle with liquid and press the nozzle for a fine mist. When the air canister is empty, it can be replaced. This is an ozone-friendly, airbrushlike tool you can purchase at painting-supply and craft stores. The sprayer functions best when the bottle is completely full; air space in the bottle can affect the evenness of the spray.

Procion MX dyes: The most versatile of the Procion dyes, these can be used for immersion dyeing, hand painting, or spraying.

Salt: Noniodized table salt may be added to an immersion dyebath. This is available in large quantities through wholesale grocers.

Scouring: Washing the fabric to remove dirt and manufacturer-applied sizing and finishes before dyeing.

Sizing: Starches and stiffeners applied to fabric so it will look better on the bolt. Sizing must be removed or it will interfere with the fabric's ability to absorb dye.

Soda ash: Sodium carbonate, the alkali used to fix Procion dyes. PRO Chem sells PRO Dye Activator, a mix that replaces soda ash and works in all geographic areas. (See "Resources" on page 156.)

Sodium alginate: A thickener that adds control in printing and painting with dyes. PRO Chem manufactures and sells PRO Thick SH for cotton and rayon, and Pro Thick F for silk. (See "Resources" on page 156.)

Synthrapol: A highly concentrated cleanser for dyed fabrics. Synthrapol is manufactured specifically for use with Procion dyes and is a surfactant—it keeps the unused dye in suspension so it can be more readily washed out.

Urea: A humectant. It makes the dyebath seem wetter to the dye molecules, facilitating the dyeing process. Urea is used primarily for hand painting and silk screening.

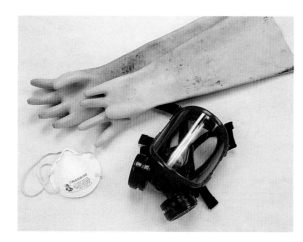

Safety Precautions

Procion dyes are considered nontoxic—they are thought to be relatively safe—but this does not mean you should neglect good housekeeping and safety habits.

❖ Wear a dust mask or respirator while mixing dye powders and always wear rubber gloves.

❖ Do not smoke, eat, or drink around the dyes.

❖ Never use equipment for cooking or food preparation if it has been used for dyeing.

❖ Label all chemicals and keep them away from children and pets.

❖ If you are considering pregnancy, are pregnant, or are nursing, be very, very careful around dyes. Consult your doctor. To be on the safe side, you may want to discontinue dyeing. Although no studies have been done on nursing mothers (for obvious reasons), the wisest attitude is "better safe than sorry." Enjoy your infant. There will be plenty of time for dyeing later.

❖ Because wet dye solution dries to dye powder, clean as you go. Wash out your sponges, rags, and mops in the washing machine. If you must sweep up dye powder, do it with a damp mop and rinse the mop in running water. If you get dye on your hands, do not use bleach to remove it. Bleach can be harmful. You can purchase Reduran™, a specially formulated hand cleaner, from a dye supplier to remove dye stains from your hands. Or use a mild soap and be patient. It is better to use your gloves so you never have to worry.

Measuring tools, buckets, and the washing machine can be easily cleaned with soap and water. Pour a cup of chlorine bleach into the rinse cycle of your washing machine if you like.

❖ Dispose of the dyebath by pouring it down the drain. Exhausted dye is about as alkaline as a normal load of laundry and poses no problem for a home septic or sewage system.

Basic Recipes

The following recipes are based on the weight of the fabric and the proportion of fabric to liquid. My standard for the latter is 1 pound—2 to 3 yards of fabric—per 1 gallon. If you want absolute accuracy, use a small scale to weigh the dry fabric. I have never weighed fabric, and I don't feel it is necessary. Just use common sense. Adjust the amount of dye powder in proportion to the weight of the fabric, and don't try to pack a dye bucket too full of fabric. Make samples and record the recipe you used and the changes you made in your notebook. Then, no matter what you do, you'll have a way to reproduce or avoid your results.

If you study the basic dye recipes, you will see similarities. For example, the immersion dyebath recipe includes dye powder, salt, soda ash, and water softener. The hand-painting or rainbow-dyeing recipe includes many of these chemicals, but the soda ash is not added to the dye-stock solution. To understand the roles various chemicals play in the dye process, read through the recipes and applications. It is easier to understand the recipes when you understand how to use the chemicals.

Because the solutions in some recipes (like the immersion dyebath) must be used at once, these recipes are based on small quantities of chemicals and fabric. If you want to dye larger pieces or quantities of fabric, increase the recipe as needed. If the solution can be stored indefinitely, the recipe is for larger quantities. You'll find that it is easy to adjust the recipes as needed once you are familiar with them.

Soda-Ash Soak

Soak the fabric before using it in a hand-painting (rainbow-dyeing) process. One gallon of warm water is enough to thoroughly saturate 2 to 3 yards of fabric.

Materials

Rubber gloves
Plastic bucket
Measuring cups and spoons
1 cup soda ash per 1 gallon
　of water

1 gallon warm (75° to 95°)
　water per pound of fabric
Fabric (prewashed)

Optional Materials

Thermometer　　　　　　　Long-handled spoon

Procedure

1. Measure the soda ash into the bucket. Add warm water. Using your gloved hand or a long-handled spoon, stir until the soda ash is completely dissolved.
2. Soak the fabric in the soda ash and water solution for 10 minutes or longer. (It takes at least 10 minutes for the fabric to absorb the soda ash. More time won't hurt.)
3. Wring the excess solution from the fabric, or spin the fabric in the washing machine.
4. Hang to dry. Do not use a clothes dryer; it will leach soda ash from the fabric. The fabric is ready to be used in a dyeing process.

Untitled Yardage by Marla Painter Ripps, 1995, San Antonio, Texas. Cotton soaked in soda ash, then hand painted with dyes.

Chemical Water

The chemicals in this recipe dissolve best when mixed in an electric blender. Do not reuse the blender to prepare food.

Materials

Rubber gloves	¾ cup urea
Measuring cups and spoons	1 teaspoon Calgon or
Electric blender or mixing	Metaphos
container and spoon	1 teaspoon Ludigol
1 quart warm (75° to 95°) water	Quart-size container with lid

Optional Materials

Thermometer	4 to 6 teaspoons sodium
	alginate (PRO Thick SH
	or F)

Procedure

1. Measure 2 cups of warm water into the blender. Put the lid on the blender and turn it to the "blend" setting.
2. Remove the center cap on the blender lid. Add the urea, Calgon or Metaphos, and Ludigol. Replace the center cap.
3. If desired, thicken the chemical water with sodium alginate. Remove the center cap on the blender lid. Measure 4 to 6 teaspoons sodium alginate into the blender. Replace the center cap. The chemical water will thicken almost immediately.
4. Pour the chemical water into a quart container and add warm water to make 1 quart. Cap the container and shake to thoroughly mix the contents. Sodium alginate looks grainy when it is added to liquid. Allow the chemical water to sit for 30 minutes (until it looks smooth) before using.

Chemical water contains all the ingredients needed to prepare dye solution for hand painting except the dye powder. I usually make a batch of chemical water without thickener and another batch with thickener so I have both on hand. (You can store chemical water in the refrigerator indefinitely.)

To prepare the dye solution for hand painting, pour ½ cup of (unthickened or thickened) chemical water into a container. Add dye powder and stir until the powder is completely dissolved. Remember to wear your dust mask or respirator and rubber gloves while working with dye powder!

You can also mix dye powder with ¼ cup of unthickened chemical water, then mix this solution with thickened chemical water until you have the desired consistency. It is easier to mix the dye powder with unthickened chemical water.

Dye Solution

I recommend using 1 teaspoon of dye powder per 1 cup of water. This should give a light to medium value. If you prefer a darker value, double the amount of dye powder.

The chemicals in this recipe dissolve best when mixed in an electric blender. Do not reuse the blender to prepare food.

Materials

Dust mask or respirator
Rubber gloves
Measuring cups and spoons
Electric blender or mixing
   container and spoon
1 cup warm (75° to 95°)
   water

2 tablespoons urea
½ teaspoon Calgon or
   Metaphos
½ teaspoon Ludigol
Fiber-reactive dye powder
   (1 to 2 teaspoons per
   cup of water)

Optional Materials

1 teaspoon sodium alginate
   (PRO Thick SH or F)
   per cup of dye solution

Thermometer

Procedure

Wear your dust mask or respirator while working with the dye powder.

1. Measure 1 cup of warm water into the blender. Put the lid on the blender and turn it to the "blend" setting.
2. Remove the center cap on the blender lid. Add the urea, Calgon or Metaphos, Ludigol, and dye powder. Replace the center cap. Blend thoroughly.

If you plan to stamp, stencil, or silk-screen the dye solution, you may want to thicken it with sodium alginate. Remove the center cap on the blender lid, add the sodium alginate, then replace the center cap. The solution will thicken almost immediately.

The thickened dye solution should be perfect for stamping, stenciling, and silk screening. Add more sodium alginate, ½ teaspoon at a time, if the solution is thinner than you like.

Sodium alginate looks grainy when it is added to dye solution. Allow the solution to sit for 30 minutes (until it looks smooth) before using.

. . . . For Inspiration . . . .

Untitled Yardage
by Marla Painter Ripps, 1995, San Antonio, Texas. Cotton soaked in soda ash, then hand painted with dyes.

Four Patch by Jane Dunnewold, 1996, San Antonio, Texas, 46" x 46". Dyed, painted, and silk-screened cotton velveteen and interfacing.

Dye Recipes

Immersion Dyeing

Use this immersion-dyeing recipe when you want to dye a length of fabric one color, with variations in value. You can overdye the fabric later for additional color, but on this first pass, you will put your fabric in one bucket of color and leave it there until the dye process is complete.

If you have never dyed before, start with 1 tablespoon of dye powder per 1 gallon of water in the dyebath. This provides medium values for most dyes. If you prefer a lighter value, halve the amount of dye powder. If you prefer a darker value, double the amount of dye powder.

Safety-supply stores sell shoulder-length rubber gloves that are ideal for stirring deep buckets of dye. If you are unable to find these gloves, use a long-handled plastic or stainless-steel spoon to stir the dyebath.

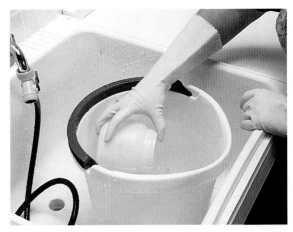

Materials

Dust mask or respirator
Rubber gloves
Measuring cups and spoons
5-gallon bucket (1 per color)
4 cups of salt per bucket
⅛ cup of soda ash per gallon
4 gallons warm (75° to 95°) water
Pint-size plastic container or jar with lid

1 tablespoon Calgon or Metaphos
Fiber-reactive dye powder (½ to 2 tablespoons per gallon)
2 to 4 yards fabric (prewashed, damp or dry) per bucket
Plastic drop cloth or plastic bags for batching
Mild detergent or Synthrapol

Optional Materials

Thermometer
Long-handled spoon

Calsolene oil

Procedure

Wear your dust mask or respirator while working with the dye powder.

1. Measure the salt and soda ash into the bucket. Add warm water. Using your gloved hand or a long-handled spoon, stir until all the chemicals are dissolved.
2. Measure 1 cup of the salt and soda-ash solution into the pint container. Add Calgon or Metaphos and dye powder. Cap the container and shake until the dye powder is completely dissolved.
3. Pour the dye solution into the bucket and stir, using your gloved hand or a long-handled spoon.
4. Immerse prewashed damp or dry fabric in the dyebath. Push it down until all the air bubbles rise to the surface. The fabric should remain submerged. Leave the fabric in the dyebath 15 minutes to 3 hours, depending on the depth of color desired. As a rule of thumb, the longer you leave the fabric immersed in the dyebath, the darker the color. Remember, though, the depth of color is also related to the amount of dye powder.

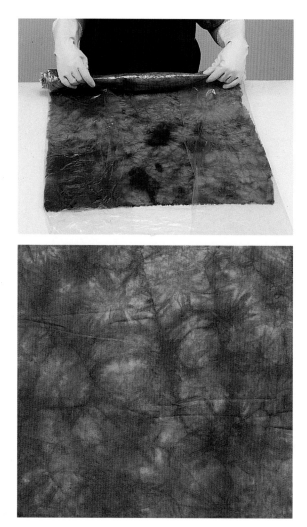

5. If you are seeking a particular value or depth of color, take the fabric out of the dye when it is slightly darker than what you desire. (Wet fabric looks darker than dry fabric.) Batch the fabric by wrapping it loosely in plastic wrap or by putting it into a plastic bag. Keep the bag warm (between 75° and 95°) for 24 to 48 hours.

If you do not have a specific color in mind, leave the fabric in the dyebath for the batching period (24 to 48 hours). When the appropriate time has elapsed, pour out the dyebath.

6. Wash your fabric in the washing machine with a mild detergent or Synthrapol. Use warm water for the first wash and rinse cycles. It may take more than one wash to remove the excess dye. After the first wash and rinse, wash the fabric in hot water until the rinse runs clear.

At no time during the dyeing process should a piece of fabric sit in a pile with other dyed fabrics, whether they are the same color or not. This can cause migration of color from one fabric to another, which is difficult to remove.

Tips and Variations for Immersion Dyeing

❖ Leaving out the water softener may enhance the variations in color (the amount of visual texture).

❖ To experiment with dyeing a length of fabric a solid color, use the washing machine. Most washing machines hold 20 gallons. Check your machine's manual to determine the amount of water it holds. You may be able to reduce the amount by selecting a smaller load setting. If you want to be exact, you can fill the washing machine, then measure out the water using a gallon-size container.

Once you know how much water you'll be using, add soda ash and salt, following the basic "Immersion Dyebath" recipe on page 51. Mix the dye-stock solution and pour it into the machine. Add ½ teaspoon of Calsolene oil per 1 gallon of water—it will help keep the dyeing even. Put your fabric in the washing machine and set the timer for the longest possible cycle. Keep track of the time and reset the cycle as necessary until you have agitated the fabric and dyebath for 1 to 2 hours, depending on the depth of color you want. When you like the color, complete the cycle. You may need to run the fabric through an additional wash cycle with Synthrapol to remove excess dye. The continuous agitation and Calsolene oil ensure an evenly dyed surface.

❖ Repeated dyeing, called overdyeing, can add depth to the surface of your fabric because of the many variations in color and pattern that occur as you manipulate and redye it. Study a color wheel (page 16) before choosing the color you will use to overdye. Colors related to the first color you dyed are more likely to blend in pleasing ways than opposites on the color wheel. In some cases, you may actually choose to dye yellow over purple, but be sure you know what will happen before you try it.

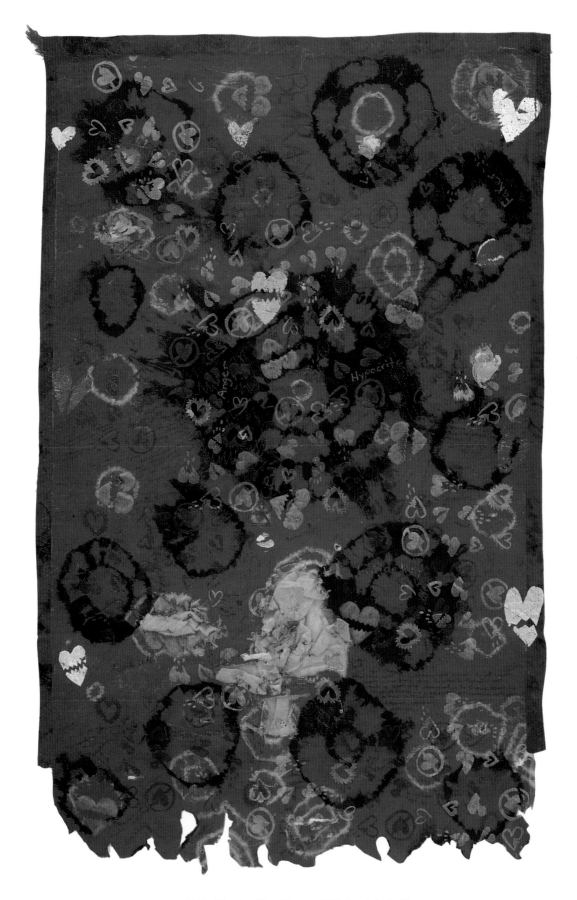

Problem #13 by Sharalyn King Johnson, 1995, San Antonio, Texas.
Dyed and overdyed cotton velveteen. Silk-screened and stamped.

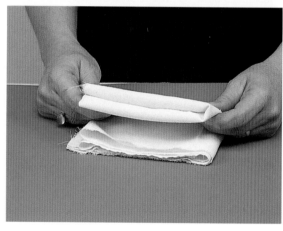

Pattern Techniques
for an Immersion Dyebath

Because we are seeking visual texture, uneven coloring and surprise patterning is a serendipitous treat rather than a problem. In fact, there are a number of ways to manipulate the fabric so predictable patterns emerge. These are variations on the tie-dye theme of the 1960s and have a loose connection to Japanese Shibori techniques you may have seen in kimono.

Folding and binding techniques are often referred to as "resists." The idea of a resist is exactly what it sounds like—tying or binding the cloth creates areas of resistance to the dye and, when successful, keeps dye from penetrating the fabric. You will encounter a number of different kinds of resists in this book. The basic concept is one of protecting areas of the fabric from dye, bleach, or paint.

The following instructions encourage you to play at folding and manipulating your fabric before you put it into the dyebath. Feel free to expand on the ideas offered here.

When dyeing and batching are completed, remove the threads, rubber bands, and other paraphernalia. Wash the fabric as described on page 56. If too much background shows to suit your taste, you can always overdye.

Materials*

Fabric
Rubber bands
Old nylon stockings
PVC pipes of various diameters
    (available at plumbing- or
    building-supply stores)

Needles and thread
Cotton string
Clamps
Small pieces of Plexiglas
Plastic clothespins (wooden
    clothespins absorb the dye)

Refer to the following procedures to determine which materials you need.

Procedures

PLEATING

Accordion-pleat the fabric just as you did a napkin when you were a kid. The cloth may first be doubled once or twice. Wrap rubber bands or string around the cloth to hold the pleats in place.

BUNCHING

Jam the entire length of cloth into a stocking leg. The tighter you pack it, the more crinkly detail you'll get.

FOLDING

Fold the fabric in half, then in half again, and again. Repeat until the cloth is folded into a tiny bundle. Wrap rubber bands around it to keep it folded.

POLE WRAP

1. Wrap the fabric around a piece of PVC pipe and secure with rubber bands. (It will be easier to scrunch if you don't wrap it too tightly.) Scrunch the fabric down around the pipe as shown.

2. Immerse the fabric and pipe in the dyebath. If some of the fabric sticks up above the dyebath and you can't scrunch it any more, use a cup to pour dye over the fabric. If your pipe is short enough, you can pour dye into a wallpaper tray and lay the pipe in the tray for the duration of the dyebath.

STITCHED RESIST

Sew running stitches in the fabric and draw them up tightly. Knot the threads. You can also machine stitch using the longest stitch setting. Remove the threads after the dyebath (before batching).

TYING CIRCLES

Use rubber bands, thread, or cotton string to make circles. Pull up a point of fabric and tighten the rubber band around it. This one is a real throwback to the 1960s.

CLAMPING

Use clamps to fold fabric around small pieces of Plexiglas. The tighter the tension, the more obvious the markings.

Be careful when using metal in a dyebath. The salt may corrode the metal and leave rust stains on the fabric. You may want to try plastic clothespins on small bundles of fabric. (They can pop off on heavier folds.)

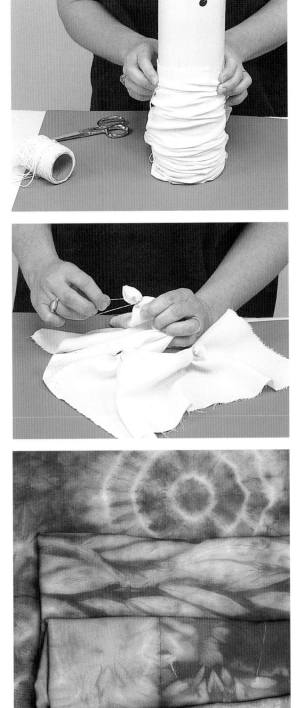

Hand Painting or Rainbow Dyeing

Rainbow dyeing is so named because this process gives you the opportunity to apply several dye colors together, as opposed to the immersion method, which limits you to one dyebath and color at a time. This technique can provide a richly colored and multihued background that is in itself pleasing. It also makes a great backdrop for additional patterning or embellishment.

Materials

Rubber gloves

Measuring cups and spoons

Soda-Ash Soak (recipe on page 51)

Plastic drop cloth

T-pins

Dye Solution (recipe on page 53)

Fabric (prewashed, damp or dry)

Foam or bristle brushes, assorted sizes

Small containers with lids for holding different colors of dye solutions

Plastic wrap or plastic sheeting

Mild detergent or Synthrapol

Optional Materials

Stretcher bars (available at art-supply stores)

Sodium alginate (PRO Thick SH or F)

Procedure

1. Prepare the soda ash soak and immerse the fabric in it for 10 minutes. You can paint on dry or damp fabric for different effects. If the fabric is damp, the brush marks will bleed slightly, giving the design a soft look. Dry fabric does not bleed as much, providing crisper, cleaner lines and images.

2. Position your fabric. Choose one of the following:

If you are painting freehand, stretch your fabric between 2 table-tops or sawhorses and pin it to the edges. Protect the floor below your work surface with a plastic drop cloth. Pull the tables or sawhorses apart so the fabric is taut.

If you are working with smaller pieces of fabric, stretch the fabric on stretcher bars and attach with T-pins. (Stretch a T-shirt over a T-shirt form.)

You can also cover a padded work table with a plastic drop cloth and pin the fabric to the tabletop. This works well if you are stamping, stenciling, or silk screening.

3. Prepare the dye solution. Small containers of dye will go a long way in this technique. Start with ½ cup of warm water per color.

4. Using foam or bristle brushes, paint the dyes on the fabric. There will be some overlap of color, especially if you are working on damp cloth. Make sure the overlap will blend into pleasing colors!

5. When you are done painting, you can batch the fabric or air-dry and steam it later. If you intend to batch a long piece of yardage, try to paint it in a place where you can leave it overnight. Cover loosely with plastic wrap so it will stay damp. The room should be warm. If you must wrap it up, lay it down on a large piece of plastic sheeting and roll it up from one end. This will keep the dyed surfaces from touching each other and prevent dye migration. Batch for 24 to 48 hours.

6. Wash your fabric in the washing machine with a mild detergent or Synthrapol. Use warm water for the first wash and rinse cycles. It may take more than one wash to remove the excess dye. After the first wash and rinse, wash the fabric in hot water until the rinse water runs clear.

Tips and Variations for Rainbow Dyeing

In addition to brushes, you can apply dye solution with a syringe, baster, toothbrush, rubber stamp, stencil, silk screen, or PreVal Sprayer or plant mister. For more control and a crisper image, thicken the dye solution by adding sodium alginate (PRO Thick SH or F). Sprinkle 1 teaspoon of sodium alginate on the surface of the dye solution and stir gently. Allow the solution to thicken for 30 minutes before you use it. If you prefer to work with a thicker dye solution, add another ½ teaspoon.

For basic instructions on stamping, stenciling, and silk screening, see "Applications" on pages 20–45. If you decide to batch the fabric after completing any of these processes, make sure it stays damp for 24 to 48 hours. To ensure good color and results, you may want to batch the fabric longer than 48 hours. Some artists who paint and stamp with dye leave the piece several weeks before washing it out. The longer the work sits, the more stable the dyes become.

❖ To experiment with a syringe or baster, use thin dye solution. Hold a paper towel under the tip of the syringe or baster to catch drips as you work. This prevents splotches.

❖ Rubber stamps are a wonderful way to apply dye solution. Stamp patterns tend to bleed on damp fabric, providing a soft look. Dry fabric provides much crisper images.

❖ Hand-cut or commercial stencils work beautifully with thickened dyes. Apply the dye solution as you would fabric paint (pages 80–81), taking care not to push dye solution under the stencil edges. You can also shade the stencil areas with different colors.

❖ Silk-screen thickened dye solution as you would fabric paint (pages 82–85). For a crisper image, use dry fabric.

❖ Create lovely effects by spraying thin dye solution with a PreVal Sprayer or plant mister. This produces a pointillist look—small dots of color blending together much like an Impressionist painting. Fill a PreVal Sprayer or plant mister with thin dye solution. Spray flat fabric or scrunch the fabric for more visual texture. Try using different dye colors. Procion fiber-reactive dyes should be sprayed outdoors or in an easy-to-clean setting. Always wear your respirator and rubber gloves when spraying dyes. Do not allow the dye solution to dry on floors, tables, or other objects; it can be difficult to remove.

Spray painting can be easily adapted to different brands and types of dye. You can substitute common household dye, such as Rit®, for Procion dye. Rit is nontoxic and easy to use. If you would prefer to use Rit, follow the package directions and mix it with hot water. Consider doubling the amount of dye in proportion to the amount of water required. Doubling the dye provides more intense colors. Rit dye does not need to be set after drying. Fabrics dyed with common household dye will not be as colorfast or washfast as those dyed with Procion dye. The important thing is that you find a product that suits your needs and provides pleasing results.

Bleach Discharge

Discharging is the chemical removal of color as a means of creating a design. Dyes and paints add color. Discharging takes color away, or in some cases, changes a fabric from one color to another.

There are a number of chemicals capable of removing dye from fabric. I use common household bleach because it is the safest and least-smelly chemical available for discharging. During the discharging process, bleach will be in contact with the fabric for a very short period of time. This means the fabric will not be damaged by the bleach any more than a load of white clothing is damaged when it runs through a wash cycle containing bleach.

When you choose fabric to discharge, keep these points in mind:

❖ Household bleach can be used on cellulose (plant) fibers, but will damage silk or wool because they are protein (animal) fibers. This may seem like an obstacle, but there are many cottons and rayons capable of discharging with wonderful results.

❖ Do not use polyester/cotton blends. Blends do not bleach well enough to warrant the time it takes to process them. Choose 100% cotton or rayon. If in doubt when you are shopping, carry a small vial of bleach with you and request a sample of the fabric. Retreat to the car and test your sample as described on page 15 before purchasing the fabric.

❖ Choose dark colors. This technique lightens fabrics. If you begin with a light-colored fabric, the change will be minimal.

❖ The heavier the weave and the fabric, the more control you have over the bleach bleeding or spreading. Smoothly woven, lightweight fabrics tend to bleed, making it harder to get a clear pattern. A heavy fabric with some "tooth" or roughness to the weave is easiest to use at first. Sand-washed rayons and rayon broadcloth are great examples.

Some colors do very unexpected things! Blues usually discharge to peach or salmon. Blacks frequently discharge to beige or brown. Spontaneity is the order of the day.

Safety Precautions

Household bleach contains chlorine and can be a dangerous chemical if misused. Read the warning label on the bottle and follow the manufacturer's guidelines. If you have heart or respiratory problems, do not work with bleach.

❖ Always work outside, if possible, or in a well-ventilated area. Protect the area surrounding your work surface with a plastic drop cloth or sheeting.

❖ Wear protective goggles and rubber gloves. If you are spraying bleach, wear a respirator.

❖ *Prewash the fabric you intend to bleach* in hot water with a mild detergent such as Synthrapol. Manufacturer's sizing frequently contains formaldehyde, which may react with bleach to produce toxic fumes.

❖ Do not smoke, eat, or drink around bleach.

❖ Label all chemicals and keep them away from children and pets.

❖ If you are considering pregnancy, are pregnant, or are nursing, be very, very careful around bleach.

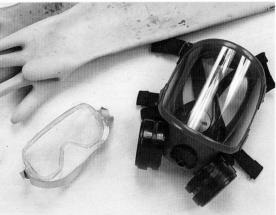

Basic Recipes

Monagum Thickener

If the fabric you are discharging is smooth and tightly woven, you may want to thicken the bleach with monagum powder. This is a modified starch gum you can use to thicken bleach for more control in stamping, stenciling, and painting. Bleach thickened with monagum powder has a paintlike consistency.

Materials

Box fan
Plastic drop cloth or sheeting
Protective goggles
Rubber gloves
Measuring cups and spoons
1 cup warm water
Mixing container and wire whisk or electric blender
3 tablespoons monagum powder
Plastic container with lid
Household bleach
Fabric scraps

Procedure

1. Pour the warm water into the mixing container or blender. Sprinkle the monagum powder onto the water and stir gently (or blend). When the thickener and water are thoroughly mixed, allow to stand for 30 minutes. The mixture should thicken considerably and become translucent. *Do not add bleach until you are ready to work.*

2. Measure ½ cup of the monagum thickener prepared in step 1 into the plastic container. Add bleach 1 tablespoon at a time until the consistency is that of a smooth paste. *Do not exceed 50% bleach.* Test the mixture on a fabric scrap to determine how quickly the bleaching action occurs. Add more bleach if desired, but never more than 50%.

You can store monagum powder indefinitely in a cool, dry place. You can store thickened monagum in the refrigerator for 6 months. Do not save the bleach/monagum mixture. The bleach gradually disintegrates the monagum thickener, making it ineffective.

Another alternative is to use sodium alginate to thicken the bleach. Some sodium alginate products work better than others, so you may need to experiment. The SH Thickener from ProChem has been most effective for me.

Measure 2 tablespoons of SH Thickener and 1 cup of bleach into a shaker bottle. Cap the bottle, then shake well to mix. Allow to sit for 15 minutes before using. Add more thickener for a denser prodcut. This will last for up to 8 hours.

Discharge Recipes

This is a very satisfying technique because the ingredients are readily available and the results are almost instantaneous. Assemble your materials before you begin. Once the bleaching action starts, you will want to work quickly. Remember to test your fabrics in advance.

You must prewash the fabric you intend to bleach. Dry and iron your fabric after washing. Dry fabric provides crisper, clearer images. In your first samples, work toward control.

I recommend working on a padded table. Cover it with a plastic drop cloth or plastic sheeting to protect the fabric. If you do not have a padded table, cover your work surface with several layers of old towels or folded muslin and a plastic drop cloth or sheeting. Cover the floor, too, if it cannot be easily cleaned.

Foam brushes work best for these processes. Do not use natural-bristle brushes, which have protein fibers that, like silk and wool, will be ruined by the bleach. Synthetic-bristle brushes don't provide enough control over the amount of bleach you are applying, so I don't generally recommend them.

Untitled Bolero *(above) by Sarah Kalvin and Jane Dunnewold, 1994, San Antonio, Texas. Discharged and hand-painted cotton velveteen. (Original pattern by Sarah Kalvin)*

Baby Bolero *(below) by Sarah Kalvin, 1995, San Antonio, Texas. Dyed silk broadcloth. Silk-screened, stenciled, and foiled. (Original pattern by Sarah Kalvin; fabric by Jane Dunnewold)*

. . . . . . For Inspiration . . . . . .

Stamping

See "Stamping Basics" on pages 20–27.

Materials

Box fan
Slightly padded work surface
Plastic drop cloth or sheeting
Protective goggles
Rubber gloves
Fabric (prewashed, dried, and ironed)

Measuring cup
Household bleach
Small container with lid for holding bleach
Foam brushes*
Hand-cut or commercial stamps

Optional Materials

Monagum powder

Remember to scale the size of your brush to the size of your stamp. Too small a brush will not adequately coat the stamp with bleach. Too large a brush will put too much bleach on your stamp.

Procedure

1. Assemble your materials and prepare your work area.

2. Stretch out the dry, ironed fabric on the work surface.

3. Fill your washing machine with cool water and set the controls so the machine will not cycle. You want it to be ready when you complete the discharge process.

4. Pour ½ to 1 cup of bleach in the small container. If your fabric is smooth and tightly woven, you may want to thicken the bleach with monagum powder. Follow the "Monagum Thickener" recipe on page 64.

5. Apply the bleach to your stamp using a foam brush. Brush enough bleach onto the stamp to moisten it. If either the brush or the stamp drips bleach, you are applying too much. This is the most common and easiest mistake. It takes very little bleach to make a crisp impression on the cloth.

6. Press the bleach-coated stamp firmly on your fabric. The discharging action will be immediate. Continue to stamp the fabric until you are happy with the pattern. If the fabric is discharging quickly, remember you can always wash out one section and dry it, then complete the rest.

7. Carefully transfer the fabric to the washing machine. Try to keep bleached areas from touching unbleached areas. You can wash several lengths of discharged fabric at once, even when the fabrics are different colors. Begin the wash cycle.

8. Hang the fabric to dry or dry it in the dryer.

9. Clean your tools with running water to remove all traces of bleach. Pour any unused bleach back into the bottle. Throw away any unused, thickened bleach.

Stenciling

Stenciling with a hand-cut or commercial stencil is particularly effective on fabrics with some texture, such as cotton velveteen, jacquard, woven rayon, and cotton. Black cotton velveteen discharges beautifully, and the texture lends itself to crisp lines. See "Stenciling Basics" on pages 28–31.

Materials

Box fan
Slightly padded work surface
Plastic drop cloth or sheeting
Protective goggles
Rubber gloves
Fabric (prewashed, dried,
  and ironed)

Hand-cut or commercial stamps
Measuring cup
Household bleach
Small container with lid for
  holding bleach
Foam and stencil brushes

Optional Materials

Spray adhesive

Monagum powder

Procedure

1. Assemble your materials and prepare your work area.

2. Stretch out the dry, ironed fabric on the work surface.

3. Fill your washing machine with cool water and set the controls so the machine will not cycle. You want it to be ready when you complete the discharge process.

4. You may want to spray the back of the stencil with spray adhesive. This helps the stencil stick to your fabric and makes your job easier. Carefully place the stencil on the fabric.

5. Pour ½ to 1 cup of bleach in the small container. If your fabric is smooth and tightly woven, you may want to thicken the bleach with monagum powder. Follow the "Monagum Thickener" recipe on page 64.

6. Dampen a foam brush with bleach. Using too much bleach will cause bleeding and fuzzy edges on your stenciled image. Carefully apply bleach to the open areas of the stencil.

    The discharging action will be immediate. Continue to stencil the fabric until you are happy with the pattern. If the fabric is discharging quickly, remember you can always wash out one section and dry it, then complete the rest.

7. Carefully transfer the fabric to the washing machine. Try to keep bleached areas from touching unbleached areas. You can wash several lengths of discharged fabric at once, even when the fabrics are different colors. Begin the wash cycle.

8. Hang the fabric to dry or dry it in the dryer.

9. Clean your tools with running water to remove all traces of bleach. Pour any unused bleach back into the bottle. Throw away any unused, thickened bleach.

Rolling

Rolling creates patterns much like the ragged or rolled wall textures popular in interiors.

Materials

Box fan
Slightly padded work surface
Plastic drop cloth or sheeting
Protective goggles
Rubber gloves
Fabric (prewashed, dried, and ironed)

Measuring cup
Household bleach
Small container with lid for holding bleach
10" x 10" square of polyester fabric

Optional Materials

Monagum powder

Procedure

1. Assemble your materials and prepare your work area.
2. Stretch out the dry, ironed fabric on the work surface.
3. Fill your washing machine with cool water and set the controls so the machine will not cycle. You want it to be ready when you complete the discharge process.
4. Pour ½ to 1 cup of bleach in the small container. If your fabric is smooth and tightly woven, you may want to thicken the bleach with monagum powder. Follow the "Monagum Thickener" recipe on page 64.
5. Wearing rubber gloves, scrunch the 10" square of polyester fabric in a roll or hot dog–like shape. Dip the roll in bleach and wring it out.
6. Roll the polyester across the surface of your fabric as if you were using a rolling pin. You can create a variety of textures with this rolling motion. Experiment.

   The discharging action will be immediate. Continue to roll the fabric until you are happy with the pattern. If the fabric is discharging quickly, remember you can always wash out one section and dry it, then complete the rest.
7. Carefully transfer the fabric to the washing machine. Try to keep bleached areas from touching unbleached areas. You can wash several lengths of discharged fabric at once, even when the fabrics are different colors. Begin the wash cycle.
8. Hang the fabric to dry or dry it in the dryer.
9. Clean your tools with running water to remove all traces of bleach. Pour any unused bleach back into the bottle. Throw away any unused, thickened bleach.

Hand Painting

Materials

Box fan
Slightly padded work surface
Plastic drop cloth or sheeting
Protective goggles
Rubber gloves
Fabric (prewashed, dried,
    and ironed)

Measuring cup
Household bleach
Small container with lid for
    holding bleach
Syringe
Paper towels

Optional Materials

Foam brushes

Small synthetic-bristle brush

Procedure

1. Assemble your materials and prepare your work area.

2. Stretch out the dry, ironed fabric on the work surface.

3. Fill your washing machine with cool water and set the controls so the machine will not cycle. You want it to be ready when you complete the discharge process.

4. Pour ½ to 1 cup of bleach in the small container.

5. Fill the syringe by inserting the tip in the bleach and slowly pulling out the plunger.

6. Gently push the plunger while moving the syringe across the fabric. Flowing motions are easiest at the start. Work with a paper towel in the hand not holding the syringe. Use the paper towel to catch the tip of the syringe as you end a line to prevent splotches.

You can also use small foam brushes to make strokes or patterns. This may be combined with the syringe lines for more variety. Use a synthetic-bristle brush to make dots, swirls, and other embellishments.

7. Carefully transfer the fabric to the washing machine. Try to keep bleached areas from touching unbleached areas. You can wash several lengths of discharged fabric at once, even when the fabrics are different colors. Begin the wash cycle.

8. Hang the fabric to dry or dry it in the dryer.

9. Clean your tools with running water to remove all traces of bleach. Pour any unused bleach back into the bottle.

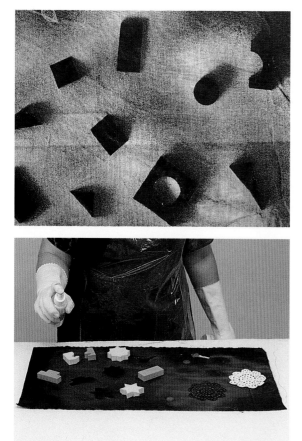

Spraying

Because you will be spraying bleach, work outside if possible. Use a box fan to increase ventilation, wear a respirator, protective goggles, and rubber gloves, and protect the area surrounding your work surface with a plastic drop cloth or sheeting.

Materials

Box fan
Plastic drop cloth or sheeting
Respirator*
Rubber gloves
Fabric (prewashed, dried, and ironed)

Leaves, keys, foam or cardboard shapes, etc.
PreVal Sprayer or plant mister
Household bleach

If you are using a quarter- or half-face respirator, wear protective goggles.

Procedure

1. Assemble your materials and prepare your work area.
2. Stretch out the dry, ironed fabric on the work surface. Arrange leaves, keys, foam or cardboard shapes—any flat thing you can think of—on the fabric. These objects will block or resist the bleach mist and create a pattern of dark impressions against the lighter, discharged surface of the cloth.
3. Fill your washing machine with cool water and set the controls so the machine will not cycle. You want it to be ready when you complete the discharge process.
4. Fill the PreVal Sprayer or plant mister with bleach.
5. Wear your respirator and rubber gloves while spraying bleach. Holding the spray bottle as upright as possible (otherwise it may leak), spray a fine mist over the entire fabric. When you remove the objects you used to block the mist, you will see the pattern beginning to discharge.

    If you like, use the resist objects as stamps. Press the bleach side down against the fabric. As the surface lightens, you will see the darker impressions of the objects alongside the lighter, shadow impressions.
6. Carefully transfer the fabric to the washing machine. Try to keep bleached areas from touching unbleached areas. You can wash several lengths of discharged fabric at once, even when the fabrics are different colors. Begin the wash cycle.
7. Hang the fabric to dry or dry it in the dryer.
8. Clean your tools with running water to remove all traces of bleach. Pour any unused bleach back into the bottle.

Serengeti (right) by Adrian Highsmith, 1994, San Antonio, Texas. Discharged black rayon collaged with burgundy silk and beaded.

Mulberry Jacket and Neckropes (left) by Renita Kuhn and Jane Dunnewold, 1993, San Antonio, Texas. Discharged and overdyed sand-washed rayon. Stamped and foiled.

For Inspiration

Pattern Techniques for Discharging

You can use resist techniques, such as pleating, rubber banding, and clamping, with bleach as well as with dye. Instead of immersing the fabric in a bucket of bleach, apply the bleach with a foam brush, or pour the bleach over the surface of the bound cloth.

Materials

Box fan
Plastic drop cloth or sheeting
Protective goggles
Rubber gloves
Fabric (prewashed, dried, and ironed)
Measuring cup

Household bleach
Small container with lid for holding bleach
Foam brush

Optional Materials*

Rubber bands
Old nylon stockings
PVC pipes of various diameters (available at plumbing- or building-supply stores)
Needles and thread

Cotton string
Clamps
Small pieces of Plexiglas
Plastic clothespins (wooden clothespins absorb the bleach)

*Refer to the procedures under "Pattern Techniques for an Immersion Dyebath" on pages 58–59 to determine which materials you need.

Procedure

1. Assemble your materials and prepare your work area.
2. Referring to "Pattern Techniques for an Immersion Dyebath" on pages 58–59, pleat, fold, bind, or clamp your fabric.
3. Fill your washing machine with cool water and set the controls so the machine will not cycle. You want it to be ready when you complete the discharge process.
4. Pour ½ to 1 cup of bleach in the small container.
5. Apply the bleach with a foam brush, or pour the bleach over the surface of the bound cloth.
6. Carefully unbind and transfer the fabric to the washing machine. Try to keep bleached areas from touching unbleached areas. You can wash several lengths of discharged fabric at once, even when the fabrics are different colors. Begin the wash cycle.
7. Hang the fabric to dry or dry it in the dryer.
8. Clean your tools with running water to remove all traces of bleach. Pour any unused bleach back into the bottle.

Tips and Variations for Discharging

❖ Using thinned fabric paints or Deka silk paints, hand paint the discharged areas of a stenciled cloth.

❖ Consider dyeing discharged fabric in one or more dyebaths.

❖ Soak discharged fabric in soda ash, then use it for hand painting or rainbow dyeing (See "Hand Painting or Rainbow Dyeing" on pages 60–61).

❖ Once in a while, fabric falls apart in the wash. Don't despair! Tear it up (using the shredding that has already occurred as your guide) and stitch the pieces onto another length of fabric.

For Inspiration

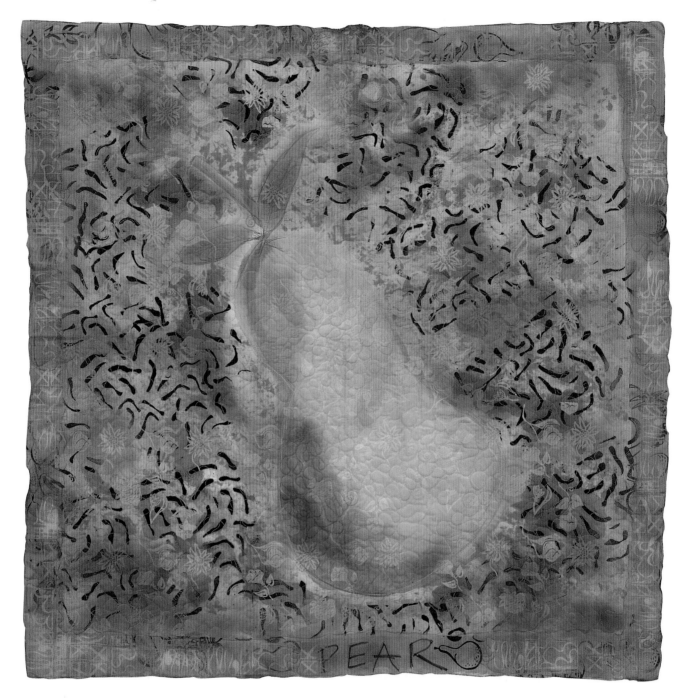

Ornamental Pear by Jane Dunnewold, 1996, San Antonio, Texas, 54″ x 54″. Hand-painted cotton. Silk-screened and stenciled.

Fabric Paints

Fabric paint is composed of pigment suspended in a waterproof, gluelike base. When paint is applied to cloth, it remains on the surface of the cloth, held there by the binding action of the paint's base. The fabric paints made today are, without exception, water based. They are related to the acrylic and latex paints used for painting fine art as well as furniture and walls. Fabric paints are formulated to be softer than traditional acrylic paints, so the hand of the fabric is not greatly altered.

In most cases, paints produce beautiful results on natural-fiber fabrics—cottons, rayons, and silks—and on natural/polyester blends of up to 50% polyester. Manufactured fabrics such as acetates, nylons, and 100% polyester may not be able to withstand the heat required to set the paints. New paint products are introduced all the time. If you are in doubt about a product, read the manufacturer's instructions and test the paint.

Paint companies make two very different kinds of fabric paint: thick and thin. Thicker paint can be stamped, silk-screened, stenciled, and hand painted. You can use this paint as is, or thin it for different applications. The thicker (or more) paint you apply, the more it will affect the hand of the fabric. There are two types of thick paint: transparent and opaque.

In transparent paints, the base dries clear—leaving transparent color on the surface of the fabric. The original color of the fabric affects the finished appearance of the cloth. What looks like smooth, dense coverage becomes a mere shadow of its former self!

Opaque paints are the opposite of transparent paints. When dry, they cover the background fabric completely. Opaque paints offer the best coverage on dark fabrics and are really your only choice on black.

Unfortunately, paint names and packaging can be confusing. Some companies refer to their fabric-paint products as "inks" or "dyes"—which is confusing as well as misleading. As a rule of thumb, any product referred to as an ink or dye is really a paint if it binds pigment to the surface of the fabric rather than bonding with the molecules in a chemical reaction. Test, test, test new paints and new products to decide whether or not a product is right for you! Trust your own judgment. When you find paints you like and companies you can rely on, support them, and let them know you think their products are great.

A paint's packaging should indicate whether the paint is transparent or opaque, but if it does not, you may have to experiment. Readily available brands include Createx®, PRO Chem, Deka, Palmer®, and Texicolor®. Other paints, including Ceramcoat®, FolkArt™, and Apple Barrel™, can be adapted for use on fabric. Textile mediums, softeners, and other additions to these paints are sold alongside them in craft stores. It is my experience that extra mediums are not needed; they are only an additional expense. See "Comparing Fabric Paints" on pages 158–59 for an analysis of paint brands and types.

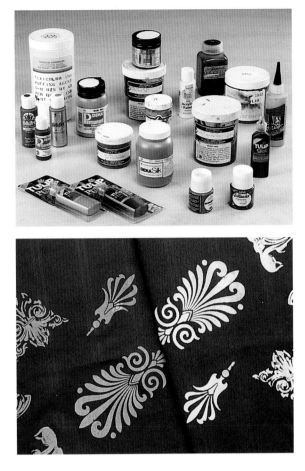

As mentioned previously, you can thin paints with water for a lighter touch or for watercolor backgrounds. You can also mix different brands and types of fabric paints. (Mixing transparent paints with opaque paints will decrease the opacity.) There are many advantages to using thick paints. You can sprinkle glitter onto damp paint or mix it into the paint; push beads, acrylic gems, stones, or found objects into thick paint before it dries; or add a puffing agent that creates a raised surface when dry.

Keep scale in mind when using thicker paints. Whether you are coating a stamp or using a stencil, choose a foam brush wide enough to work efficiently. If you are painting freehand, use a brush scaled to the image you are creating. The less paint on the brush, the more control you will have over your results.

Thick applications of paint are not always desirable or suitable for a particular process, so some paint

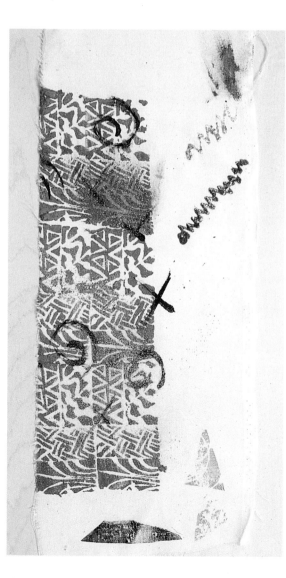

companies offer thinner versions. These paints have a watercolorlike consistency. If you like a light touch, bright color, and virtually no change in the hand of the fabric, you will love these paints. They are terrific for coloring backgrounds and brushing over resists, as well as for spraying with a PreVal Sprayer. Unlike thick paints thinned with water, thin paints do not separate because they are formulated to stay in permanent suspension. You can also stamp and stencil thin paints for a soft-edge look. Brand names include Deka Silk Paint and Peintex®.

Safety Precautions

Fabric paints are an extremely safe, but permanent, medium. Wear old clothes when you work. You may want to wear rubber gloves to protect your hands.

Fabric Paint Recipes

Choosing a selection of thick and thin fabric paints and using them to make samples is the most efficient way to learn about the various paints and their differences. While all paints are similar in content, variations do exist. Some paints are undeniably higher quality than others, as evidenced by their smooth consistency, appearance, feel when dry, and price. Different projects require different paints and

approaches. This is one of those wonderful opportunities to play and learn at the same time!

❖ Keep containers tightly sealed so paints don't dry out. Mix colors and brands freely, but remember to label your containers so you can duplicate favorite recipes later.

❖ Choose a fabric with a smooth, even weave and surface. Pebbly texture or loose weave will break up your image. Always work on dry, ironed fabric.

❖ Clean your tools immediately after you have finished painting. Fabric paints dry quickly, and dry paint ruins brushes, containers, and silk screens. Soap and water cleanup is easy as long as the paint has not dried.

❖ Always read the manufacturer's instructions for setting or curing paints, as products may vary. The majority of paints will cure in a week's time without any effort on your part. But if in doubt, use an iron or dryer to cure the paints. When you have finished painting, allow the paints to dry for 24 hours. In general, set paints by ironing the cloth on the wrong side, with the iron on the cotton setting. Steam may cause bleeding, although this is rare. Iron for 2 minutes. You can also put the fabric in the dryer and tumble on high heat for 30 minutes.

Stamping, stenciling, and silk screening are easier on a slightly padded work surface. If you do not have a padded table, pad your work table with old towels or folded muslin. If desired, protect the work surface with a plastic drop cloth or plastic sheeting.

Ornamental Apple by Jane Dunnewold,
1996, San Antonio, Texas, 54" x 40".
Hand-painted, silk-screened, and stenciled cotton.

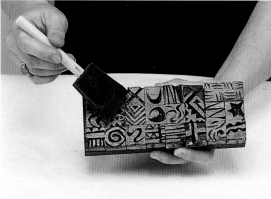

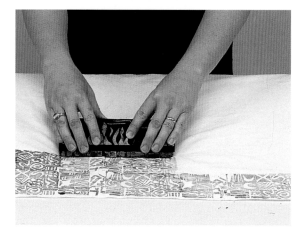

Stamping

See "Stamping Basics" on pages 20–27.

Materials

Slightly padded work surface
Fabric (prewashed, dried, and ironed)
Thick and thin fabric paints

Shallow container(s) for paint
Foam brushes in several sizes
Hand-cut or commercial stamps
Toothbrush for cleanup

Optional Materials

Rubber gloves
Plastic spoons for mixing paint

Plastic containers to mix and store custom colors

Procedure

1. Assemble your materials and prepare your work area.
2. Stretch out the dry, ironed fabric on the work surface.
3. Pour a small amount of paint into a shallow container. It does not take much paint.
4. Using a foam brush, lightly coat the stamp with paint. Too much paint will blur the image when it is printed. Never dip the stamp into the paint; you cannot control the amount or evenness of paint.
5. Press the paint-coated stamp firmly on your fabric, pushing into the padded surface. Be careful not to move the stamp sideways, as the image will smear.

   Check the imprint. If it is smeared, you moved your hand. If it is pale, you did not apply enough paint. If it is blurred, you may have used too much paint. A good image looks clear and clean. Continue stamping until you are happy with the pattern.

6. Remember to clean stamps promptly. Use an old toothbrush and warm water to scrub all paint residue from the crevices.

7. Allow the paint to dry for 24 hours. Follow the manufacturer's instructions for setting the paints. This generally involves ironing at high heat for several minutes. Iron the wrong side of your fabric.

8. Wash the fabric in the washing machine, using warm water and a mild detergent.

9. Hang the fabric to dry or dry it in the dryer.

Tips and Variations
for Stamping with Fabric Paints

- Play with color. Pour small amounts of several compatible colors into your paint dish. Dip the brush in one or more colors and apply it to the stamp. You can color-mix on the surface as you coat the stamp.

- Work with color progression. Stamp one color for awhile, then gradually switch to another color by mixing as described above.

- Overstamp. Print the fabric with a pattern going one direction, then use the same stamp or another one to print a pattern in another color going another direction. There are many variations on this theme.

- If you intend to make stamping the focus of a piece, keep scale in mind. The design won't be very interesting if your images are all the same size. Vary the size of the stamps you use in addition to varying the color.

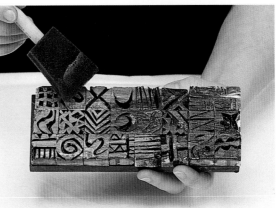

- Make several companion lengths of cloth, using the same stamps but altering the color and/or arrangement. Three ½-yard lengths stamped with coordinating colors and patterns make a lovely blouse or skirt.

- Use found objects as stamps. Old keys, leaves, and sliced vegetables are examples of objects that make interesting stamps.

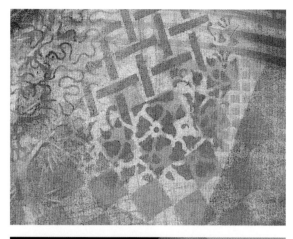

Stenciling

See "Stenciling Basics" on pages 28–31.

Materials

Slightly padded work surface
Fabric (prewashed, dried, and ironed)
Spray adhesive
Hand-cut or commercial stencils

Thick and thin fabric paints
Shallow container(s) for paint
Stencil brushes in assorted sizes and/or synthetic or sea sponges

Optional Materials

Rubber gloves
Plastic spoons for mixing paint

Plastic containers to mix and store custom colors

Procedure

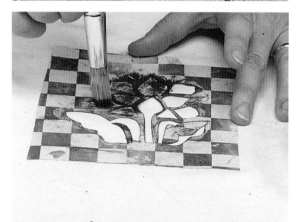

1. Assemble your materials and prepare your work area.
2. Stretch out the dry, ironed fabric on the work surface.
3. Spray the back of the stencil with spray adhesive. This helps the stencil stick to your fabric and makes your job easier. Do not overspray, as adhesive may come off the stencil onto your fabric. Carefully position the stencil and press gently on the fabric.
4. Pour a small amount of paint into a shallow container. It does not take much paint.
5. Daub your brush or sponge up and down in the paint until the bottom is coated. Too much paint blurs the image. Make sure the paint is evenly distributed on the brush by "pouncing" the brush up and down on a piece of scrap fabric before you begin.

6. Begin in the middle of your stencil, in the largest open area. Apply the paint in the up-and-down motion. Try not to glide the paint over the open areas—paint may get under the edges of the stencil, blurring the image.

Don't try to load the brush with paint in order to fill the shape quickly. Instead, apply several even coats rather than one thick coat. The drier the brush, the easier it is to make a clear image.

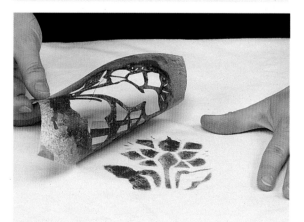

7. When you have filled all the open areas of the stencil, peel off the stencil, working from one corner as shown. Reposition the stencil and repeat if desired.
8. It is a good idea to clean the stencil every two or three applications so paint does not seep onto the side with the spray adhesive. Clean the stencil by laying it flat in the sink and sponging it gently with warm water. Store it carefully in an upright position.

9. Allow the paint to dry for 24 hours. Follow the manufacturer's instructions for setting the paint. This generally involves ironing at high heat for several minutes. Iron the wrong side of your fabric.

10. Wash the fabric in the washing machine, using warm water and a mild detergent.

11. Hang the fabric to dry or dry it in the dryer.

Tips and Variations
for Stenciling with Fabric Paints

❖ Sponge more than one color over the stencil at a time. Two or more shades of green dabbed onto a leaf shape, for instance, provides subtle shading not possible with one color.

❖ When the first stenciled image has dried, reposition the stencil and repeat the same image in a second color. This can be repeated several times to add a sense of depth and shading.

❖ When the first image has dried, reposition the stencil so it is slightly off-center from the first image. Using a second color, apply paint to the edge of the image only. This gives the appearance of a shadow on one side of your image and adds a sense of depth.

❖ When the first image has dried, use a brush or fabric marker to draw in details such as veins on leaves or shading on flower petals.

❖ Use a stencil to discharge the color from a dark fabric, then hand color the lightened areas using thinned fabric paints. This is especially effective on cotton velveteens.

❖ Stencil thinned fabric paint onto a textured fabric such as velveteen, suiting- or broadcloth-weight rayon, or cotton. The image will bleed and blur slightly because the paint is thin. When the image dries, use the same stencil again, this time applying thick paint in a compatible color. The effect will again be one of depth and contrast.

Silk Screening

You can silk-screen in a small work space—even with long lengths of yardage—by working in sections. Allow paint to dry, then move to another section of the cloth to continue printing. It is much easier, however, to have a large table that accommodates a yard or more at a time. If you must work small, consider working with fabric in lengths less than two yards.

Silk screening is not hard, but fabric texture and your ability to apply pressure affect the printing process. Always, always do a test run on scrap fabric prior to printing the real thing! See "Silk-Screening Basics" on pages 32–45.

Materials

Slightly padded work surface*
T-pins
Fabric (prewashed, dried, and ironed)
Silk screen, taped and prepared with the design you plan to use

Assorted thick fabric paints
Squeegee to fit the silk-screen frame
Soft brush or sponge for cleanup

Optional Materials

Rubber gloves

Plastic spoon

*A padded table is preferable because you can stick pins straight down into it. (For building instructions, see page 11.) If you do not have a padded table, pad your work table with old towels or folded muslin. Make sure the padding is smooth; creases or wrinkles will show up on the fabric when you print. Cover the temporary padding with an old sheet.

Procedure

1. Smooth out your fabric on the padded work table. Use the T-pins to pin the fabric to the padding. If you do not have a padded table, pin the fabric to the temporary work surface. (The fabric tends to stick to the screen after you print an image; pinning the cloth keeps it from lifting up when you remove the screen.)

2. Position the screen in the area where you want to begin printing. I usually start at one end of a length and work across to the other end. *You cannot print images side by side;* the wet paint from the image you printed last will smear onto the bottom of the silk-screen frame and mess up the fabric when you move it. If you want to print a design that repeats side by side or up and down, you must leave spaces between images (like a checkerboard), wait for the paint to dry, then go back and fill in the spaces.

3. Stand so you can pull the squeegee toward your body when you are printing. Pushing the squeegee away from your body or standing so you squeegee back and forth across the image changes the tension. The least jerky, most consistent tension—that of pulling the squeegee toward your body—provides the smoothest, most consistent printed image.

4. Pour or spoon a bead (about 2 tablespoons) of paint across the top of the silk screen—along the 1" edge of tape.

5. Hold the screen against the fabric with one hand. Using the other hand, pull the squeegee toward you, across the surface of the screen. Hold the squeegee as perpendicular to the screen as possible.

The printing action applies the paint and forces it through the open areas of the mesh. If your screen is fairly large, you may need two hands to squeegee. Having a companion to hold the screen in place is a good idea if you are working with a big frame.

6. It may take more than one pass to force enough paint through the mesh to make an evenly printed image. Instead of pushing paint back across the mesh, use the squeegee to scoop up the excess paint closest to you and put it back at the top of the frame. Then squeegee toward yourself again. Two or three passes should result in a complete image.

7. Pick up the screen by carefully lifting one side from the fabric. Reposition it and continue printing if desired.

8. You must work quickly when you are silk screening. It is very difficult to remove paint that has dried on the surface of a screen. When you finish screening the project at hand, wash the screen with warm water and mild soap. Use a soft brush to scrub the screen. You should be able to remove every bit of paint—not only from the mesh of the screen, but from the corners and crevices of the frame as well. A properly exposed screen is very durable and can withstand a fair amount of scrubbing.

Do not be alarmed if you can still see color when you finish cleaning the screen. The mesh is easily discolored by the paint. Hold the screen up to the light to double-check. You should not see opaque areas of paint blocking the light.

If necessary, rub the paint with lacquer thinner or turpentine. Unfortunately, lacquer thinner and turpentine may dissolve the emulsion as well as the paint. In this case, reclaim the screen with bleach (page 42) and start over. In a worst-case scenario, the paint will not come off. If this happens, cut the mesh off the frame and rescreen the frame with new mesh. Beware of fast-drying artist's acrylics and glitter products! They can wreak havoc on a silk screen.

9. Allow the screen to air-dry before printing again. If you are anxious to continue printing, lean the screen in front of a fan. It will dry quickly. Resist the impulse to use the screen while it is damp. You may lose part of your image if you don't let it dry thoroughly.

10. Allow the paint to dry for 24 hours. Follow the manufacturer's instructions for setting the paints. This generally involves ironing at high heat for several minutes. Iron the wrong side of your fabric.

11. Wash the fabric in the washing machine, using warm water and a mild detergent.

12. Hang the fabric to dry or dry it in the dryer.

Troubleshooting

If the image did not print:

❖ *Not enough pressure was used during squeegeeing. Try pushing down more firmly as you print.*

❖ *The squeegee was held at too narrow an angle to be effective. Keep it as straight up and down as possible.*

❖ *Not enough passes were made to fill the image with paint. Experiment with a fabric scrap; pay attention to the number of passes needed to fill the image.*

❖ *The paint may be drying on the screen and blocking the mesh. Get to the sink as fast as you can and clean that screen!*

It is possible to go back to an incomplete image and salvage it. Resist the impulse to put the screen back down and squeegee another pass or two. This may smear the image. Instead, wait for the paint to dry. After the paint dries, it will be easy to reposition the screen. Line it up on the incomplete image by looking through the mesh and using the part that did print as your guide. When you have realigned the image exactly, print it again.

If the image smeared:

❖ *The paint may be too thin. Use a thicker paint.*

❖ *You may have moved the screen slightly. Make sure the screen doesn't move during printing.*

❖ *You may have picked up paint on the back of the screen. Check it and wash if needed.*

❖ *You may have printed so many times that paint has seeped onto the back of the screen. Clean the screen before continuing.*

❖ *The mesh on your screen may not be the right size for fabric printing. If you do not know what size the mesh is and the problem continues, consider re-screening the frame in a 10xx or 12xx mesh.*

❖ *You may be passing the squeegee over the image too many times. Try squeegeeing fewer times on each print. In general, the smoother the fabric, the fewer passes it will take to print your image.*

Tips and Variations
for Silk Screening with Fabric Paints

❖ Print a design in one color. Wait for it to dry, then overprint in a second compatible color. Print the second color at random, overlapping the first design.

❖ Sprinkle loose glitter over the wet paint.

❖ Spoon two or more colors onto the screen at once and squeegee them together. This creates lovely blended effects.

❖ Print the design. Wait for it to dry. Block off part of the silk screen temporarily with masking tape and newspaper. Print the partial design over the dry design.

Hand Painting

Hand painting intimidates some of us more than stamping, stenciling, and silk screening combined. A little voice says we can't just pick up a brush and paint—we need a stamp, a stencil, or a screen to shape the design. If you balk at the idea of painting freehand, approach it as playtime. Painting with a brush gets easier the more you do it, becoming a pleasure instead of a chore.

To begin, you may want to work on a small piece of fabric. A smoother-weave fabric allows more detail than a heavier-weave fabric. Always iron the fabric; wrinkles break up the design.

Materials

Slightly padded work surface*

Fabric (prewashed, dried, and ironed)

Plastic spoons

Thick and thin fabric paints in different colors

Shallow tray for paint

Assorted brushes (foam brushes, small and large bristle brushes)

Container for water

If you do not have a padded table, pad your work table with old towels or folded muslin. You do not need a great deal of padding, but you do need an absorbent background.

Optional Materials

Rubber gloves

Metallic paints

Glitter paints

Procedure

1. Assemble your materials and prepare your work area.
2. Stretch out the dry, ironed fabric on the work surface.
3. Spoon several colors of fabric paint into a shallow tray. Mix colors in the tray to broaden your palette.
4. Begin by trying out different kinds of brushes. Using a foam brush, make several wide swipes on your fabric. Make a few curlicues or circles with a medium bristle brush. Make a series of dots with a small brush. Thin the paints slightly with water and continue playing with the paint on your fabric.
5. When you have finished, wash all tools in warm water.
6. Allow the paint to dry for 24 hours. Follow the manufacturer's instructions for heat setting the paints. This generally involves ironing at high heat for several minutes on the wrong side of your fabric.

Tips and Variations
for Hand Painting with Fabric Paints

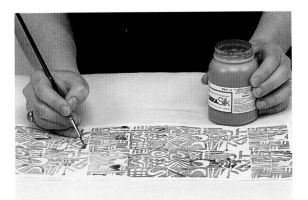

❖ You are limited only by your imagination. Try a metallic paint or thin a glitter paint. Paint mixed with glitter makes a nice, sparkly background.

❖ Blend thinned paint on the fabric surface for a hint of background color.

❖ Combine hand painting—swirls, dots, lines—with stamped patterns.

❖ To paint a recognizable object, pick a flower or a piece of fruit. Study it. Looking at the actual object can teach you a great deal about color, texture, and scale.

❖ Scale, scale, scale! If you want to paint fine detail (little flowers and leaves), use a very fine brush. If you are filling larger areas with color, use a larger brush. Choosing the right brush and limiting the amount of paint you use will give you greater control.

· · · · · · · · · · · · · · For inspiration · · · · · · ·

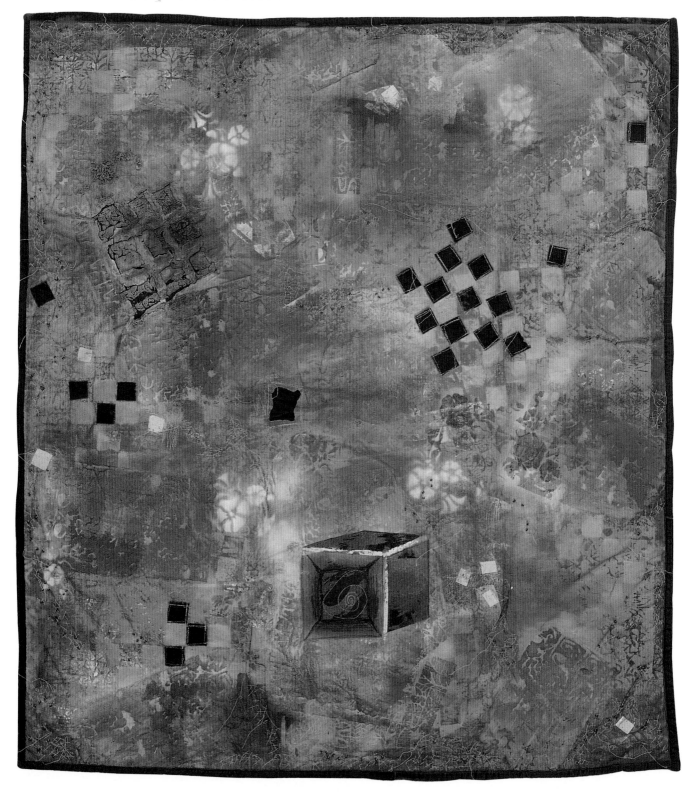

Pandora's Box *by Jane Dunnewold, 1996, San Antonio, Texas, 54" x 60".*
Dyed cotton. Silk-screened, stamped, and foiled. Embellished with velvet,
painted interfacing, and beads.

Puff Painting

Puff paints are like fabric paints, but you add a puffing agent to the paint so it will puff when heat is applied. The puffing agent is composed of tiny, plastic bubbles that expand when heated, creating the raised surface. You can apply puff paints like other fabric paints; they work well for stamping, stenciling, silk screening, and hand painting.

Puff paints are prepackaged by a number of companies and sold in very small containers at craft stores. These paints are often used to decorate T-shirts, tennis shoes, etc. The small size of the packaging makes the paint expensive and somewhat inconvenient to use. If you are stamping or stenciling, squeeze the paint out of the tube to work. You can also draw freehand with the tube.

To experiment with silk screening or stenciling on a larger scale, consider ordering puffing agent from the Texicolor Corporation. (See "Resources" on page 156.) Loose puffing agent looks like mashed-potato flakes and comes in pint- and quart-size containers. Add 4 to 6 ounces of puffing agent to 1 cup of fabric paint for a wonderful puff paint that can be silk screened and stenciled.

Puff paint invariably lightens after it is puffed. For medium or dark values, experiment with mixing colors slightly darker than you want them to be. Make labeled samples for reference.

Fabric texture is an important consideration when you are working with puff paint. Smoother fabrics allow for greater detail than rougher fabrics, which tend to break up the puffed surface. Puff paint can be used with any fiber content, so long as the fabric can withstand the heat necessary to create the puffing action.

Materials

6 ounces puffing agent
1 cup fabric paint
Small mixing container and spoon

Steam iron, portable travel steamer, or heat gun

Optional Materials
Small food scale

Procedure

1. Mix puffing agent and fabric paint, following the manufacturer's instructions. The suggested amount of puffing agent is 6 ounces per 1 cup of paint. Adding less or more agent will influence the degree of puffing that occurs when the paint is heated. I prefer a less-raised surface, so I use 4 ounces of puffing agent per 1 cup of paint.
2. Apply the puff paint as you would apply fabric paint in any process. *Do not dilute the paint; it diminishes the puffing effect.*
3. Allow the paint to dry to the touch.

Silver Fish by Shelly Kyle, 1994, San Antonio, Texas. Dyed cotton. Silk-screened, foiled, and puff-painted.

. . . . . For inspiration . . . .

4. When the paint is dry, heat the right side of the fabric. You can use a steam iron, a portable travel steamer, or a heat gun. If you use a steam iron, hold the iron slightly above the surface of the cloth and push the steam button. Shots of steam combined with the iron's heat puff the paint quickly. It will raise before your eyes. If you use a portable travel steamer, hang the fabric, then steam. If you use a heat gun, hold the gun close to, but not touching, the fabric.

5. Care for puff paints by machine washing on gentle and hanging to dry, or by dry cleaning. *Do not put cloth painted with puff paint in the dryer. The puffing action will be intensified, pulling the cloth out of shape.*

Troubleshooting

Sometimes puff paint expands too much, looking like popcorn on the surface of the cloth. If this happens, you either used too much puffing agent or heated the paint too much.

Tips and Variations for Working with Puff Paints

❖ Add puffing agent to white paint and apply. When the paint is dry and has been puffed and cooled, overpaint it by spraying it with thinned fabric paint, or apply paint to the puffed surface with a brush. For a wonderful leatherlike look, paint metallic paint over puff paint.

❖ Sprinkle loose glitter over damp puff paint. The glitter becomes imbedded as the paint dries.

❖ Add gems, beads, acrylic stones, and found objects to the wet puff paint. When you puff the paint, the objects become imbedded.

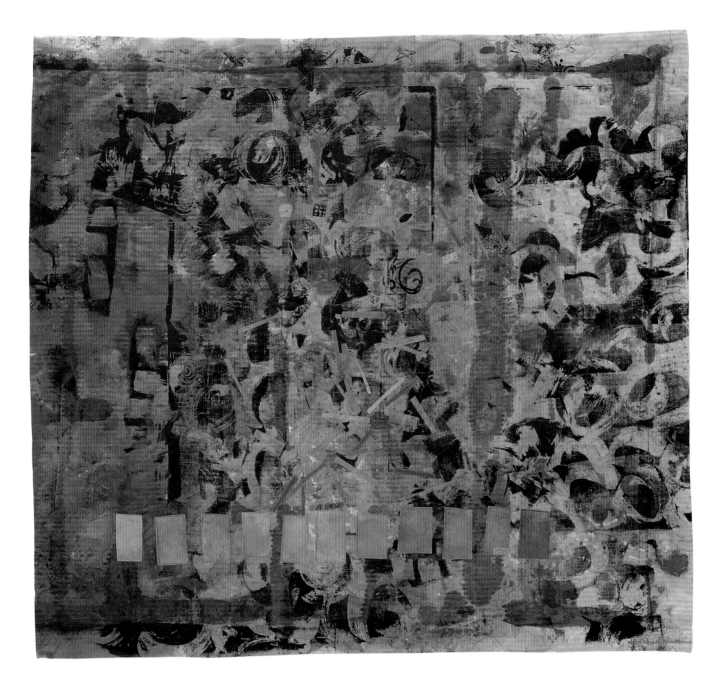

Ordering Chaos III by Jane Dunnewold, 1996, San Antonio, Texas, 65" x 54". Hand-painted cotton. Silk-screened. Embellished with hand-painted interfacing.

Human Imprint #1 *by Jane Dunnewold, 1993, San Antonio, Texas, 60" x 44". Silk treated with a water-based resist and hand painted with Deka Silk paint. Silk-screened. Embellished with copper tacks.*

Water-Based Resists

Water-based resists do just what their name implies. Their starches or soluble gluelike components penetrate the fibers and, after drying, resist dye, thinned paint, and bleach. When the fabric is washed, the resist rinses out—leaving a permanent pattern. Using a water-based resist increases your ability to develop contrast and depth by layering patterns on the surface of your fabric.

Water-based resists are a tremendously versatile patterning tool because they can be used with a variety of processes and techniques. This versatility, coupled with their ability to wash out entirely, ensures their place in your repertoire of patterning skills.

Resists

There are many ways of applying water-based resists to fabric, including stamping, stenciling, and hand painting. No matter what application technique you choose, all water-soluble resists work the same way. They seep into the fibers of the fabric and, once dry, temporarily inhibit the ability of those fibers to absorb other fluids. *The resist must dry for 24 hours before you apply dye, paint, or bleach.*

Your fabric choice will contribute greatly to your success or failure. Medium- to heavyweight fabrics, such as velvet and velveteen, shantung (wild) silk, slubby linen, and cotton, may not give good results because it is more difficult for the resists to penetrate their heavier fibers. Lighter-weight fabrics, such as cotton, rayon, silk habotai, broadcloth, and silk Charmeuse, work very well. A silk noil usually requires more than one application of resist before it is adequately saturated. If you are concerned about the weight and weave of your fabric, conduct an experiment with the resist on one corner prior to treating the entire length. To start, choose a lightweight rayon, silk, or cotton. Remember to prewash your fabric in hot, soapy water to remove sizing. Dry and iron the fabric before applying a resist.

The resists discussed here are water-based products. This means they are water soluble. I work with Deka Silk Resist, Elmer's® Glue Gel™, Inko Resist Paste, potato starch, Presist, Silkpaint® Resist, and Speedball Drawing Fluid. Each has slightly different requirements for its use. Elmer's Glue Gel and Speedball Drawing Fluid are nontraditional products I have experimented with extensively. In most cases, I have had good, reliable results. However, Speedball Drawing Fluid once permanently tinted a length of raw silk pale blue. Moral of the story? If you really care about how the product is going to work on your piece of fabric, test it first! Refer to the glossary on page 94 to determine which resist will work best with your desired technique and fabric.

When you plan your project, remember that a resist protects the background color of the fabric. If your background color is white or beige, any color added over the resist will probably be appealing. If your background fabric has been dyed or is some color other than white or beige, that hue will affect the color the cloth becomes when it is overdyed or painted. Check your color wheel and do a small test sample to prevent an unpleasant surprise!

Also keep in mind that you must be able to wash out what you use to color the fabric—dyes, paints, or bleach—and the resist. Fiber-reactive dyes work well with water-based resists. You can use dye solution as is or thicken it for more control. You cannot use fabric prepared with a water-based resist in an immersion dye bath; the resist will dissolve. Also, do not steam-set fabric prepared with a water-based resist.

Heavy fabric paints do not work well with water-based resists because they encase the resist and make it difficult to remove. You can thin heavy paints with water, but it is better to purchase fabric paints in a premixed, thinned-down formula. These paints do not separate when stored and do not clog sprayers.

Household bleach and water-based resists work very well together. Dark fabric provides the most dramatic results. Apply the resist, allow it to dry, then mist bleach across the fabric. The result is a dark pattern on a light background.

Glossary of Water-Based Resist Products

Deka Silk Resist: *A fairly thin, clear resist. It is specifically formulated for lightweight silks, but you can use it with other types of fabric as well. Deka Silk Resist does not penetrate medium- to heavyweight fabrics.*

Elmer's Glue Gel: *Not the resist of choice for extensive applications, but it can't be beat for fine-line drawings, scribbles, and doodles. Packaged in a small, school-size bottle.*

Inko Resist Paste: *Made from the root of the casaba plant and very thick in consistency. Inko is a good, all-around resist. It is terrific on light- to medium-weight fabrics and does a better job than most on heavyweight fabrics. It resists bleach well.*

Potato-starch resist: *Inexpensive with easy-to-control consistency—make it as thick or thin as you need. Make your own resist from instant mashed-potato flakes and liquid starch, following the recipe on page 96. Potato-starch resist works well with dyes, paints, and bleach. It coats the fabric when applied thickly and works well on heavyweight fabrics. It must be refrigerated and used within a week because it spoils easily.*

Presist: *One of the best all-around resists on the market. Presist provides crisp, clear patterns on light- to medium-weight fabrics and also works well on heavyweight fabrics if you work it into the fabric. Although it is expensive, Presist is the best water-based resist for working with fiber-reactive dyes.*

Silkpaint Resist: *A clear, water-based resist that can be diluted or used straight from the bottle. Although it doesn't have much staying power on medium- to heavyweight fabric, it works great on lightweight silk, rayon, and cotton. It does not resist bleach as well as some other products.*

Speedball Drawing Fluid: *Intended for use as a resist in the preparation of silk screens. It works equally well as a resist on light- to medium-weight fabrics. It can bleed if too much paint, dye, or bleach is applied and, as mentioned, may permanently tint silk noil. It resists bleach well.*

Spirit Dancers: Earth (above) by Beth Kennedy, 1994, Austin, Texas, 48" x 50". Dyed and overdyed cotton. Silk-screened and foiled. Machine-embroidered and quilted. Right, detail of "Spirit Dancers: Earth." (Photo by Libby Lehman)

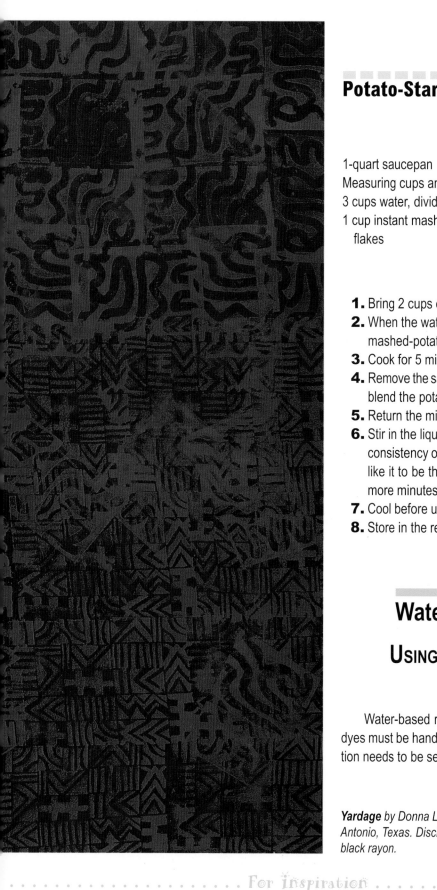

Basic Recipes

Potato-Starch Resist

Materials

1-quart saucepan
Measuring cups and spoons
3 cups water, divided
1 cup instant mashed-potato
flakes

Long-handled spoon
Electric or hand blender
1 tablespoon liquid starch

Procedure

1. Bring 2 cups of water to boil in the saucepan.
2. When the water is boiling, turn down the heat to medium and add the mashed-potato flakes.
3. Cook for 5 minutes, stirring frequently.
4. Remove the saucepan from the heat. Using the electric or hand blender, blend the potato mixture for 3 minutes.
5. Return the mixture to the heat. It should be very smooth at this point.
6. Stir in the liquid starch. If the mixture is thick enough (it should be the consistency of wallpaper paste), heat it again only briefly. If you would like it to be thinner, add the remaining 1 cup of water and cook for 5 more minutes. The mixture will thicken slightly as it cools.
7. Cool before using.
8. Store in the refrigerator; it spoils easily.

Water-Based Resist Recipes

USING WATER-BASED RESISTS WITH FIBER-REACTIVE DYES

Water-based resists work beautifully with fiber-reactive dyes, but the dyes must be hand painted on the fabric. Remember that any dye application needs to be set by batching.

Yardage by Donna LoMonaco, 1995, San Antonio, Texas. Discharged and overdyed black rayon.

Stamping

See "Stamping Basics" on pages 20–27.

Materials

Slightly padded work surface
Plastic drop cloth or sheeting
Respirator
Rubber gloves
Fabric (prewashed, dried, and ironed)
½ to 1 cup water-based resist

Shallow container for resist
Hand-cut or commercial stamps
Foam brushes
Dye Solution (recipe on page 53)
PreVal Sprayer or plant mister
Mild detergent or Synthrapol

Procedure

1. Assemble your materials and prepare your work area.
2. Stretch out the dry, ironed fabric on the work surface.
3. Pour the resist into a shallow container.
4. Apply the resist to your stamp using a foam brush. Brush enough resist onto the stamp to moisten it. If either the brush or the stamp drips resist, you are applying too much. You need enough resist to penetrate the fabric, but not so much that you can't make a clear image.
5. Press the stamp on the fabric. Lift a corner of the fabric to see if the resist penetrated. If the resist sits only on the front of the fabric, it will not adequately block the dye. If necessary, reapply resist until the pattern shows on the back. Allow to dry for 24 hours.
6. Clean your tools. Pour any unused resist back into the bottle.
7. Mix the dye solution. If desired, thicken the dye with sodium alginate. Thick dye residue readily washes away when the resist is rinsed out.
8. Fill the PreVal Sprayer or plant mister with dye solution. (If you thickened the dye, use a foam brush to apply it.)
9. Wear your respirator and rubber gloves while spraying dye. Mist the dye solution across the fabric. For deep color, apply the dye in several thin coats. Avoid soaking the fabric. If you apply too much dye solution, it may liquefy the resist. You can also apply dye solution with a foam brush, but be very careful not to soak the fabric.

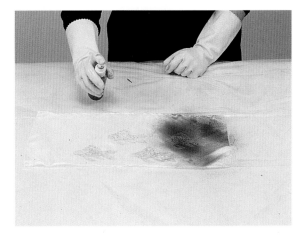

10. Cover the damp, dye-coated fabric with a piece of plastic sheeting. If you must move the fabric while it is batching, roll it carefully in the plastic. Keep the fabric at room temperature (70° or more) for at least 24 hours.
11. Rinse excess dye from the fabric, then wash in warm water with a mild detergent or Synthrapol. If desired, air-dry the fabric after batching for 24 hours and rinse and wash later. Waiting several days will not hurt the fabric and may actually help set the color.
12. Hang the fabric to dry or dry it in the dryer.
13. Clean your tools with running water.

Stenciling

See "Stenciling Basics" on pages 28–31.

Materials

Slightly padded work surface
Plastic drop cloth or sheeting
Respirator
Rubber gloves
Fabric (prewashed, dried,
  and ironed)
½ to 1 cup water-based resist

Shallow container for resist
Foam or bristle brushes
Hand-cut or commercial stencils
Dye Solution (recipe on page 53)
PreVal Sprayer or plant mister
Mild detergent or Synthrapol

Optional Materials

Spray adhesive

Procedure

1. Assemble your materials and prepare your work area.
2. Stretch out the dry, ironed fabric on the work surface.
3. You may want to spray the back of the stencil with spray adhesive. This helps the stencil stick to your fabric and makes your job easier. Carefully place the stencil on the fabric.
4. Pour the resist into a shallow container.
5. Coat a foam brush with resist. Carefully apply the resist in the open areas of the stencil. Saturate the open areas completely. Lift a corner of the fabric to see if the resist penetrated through the fabric. If the resist sits only on the front of the fabric, it will not adequately block the dye. If necessary, reapply resist until the pattern shows on the back. Allow to dry for 24 hours.
6. Clean your tools. Pour any unused resist back into the bottle.
7. Mix the dye solution. If desired, thicken the dye with sodium alginate. Thick dye residue readily washes away when the resist is rinsed out.
8. Fill the PreVal Sprayer or plant mister with dye solution. (If you thicken the dye, use a foam brush to apply it.)

9. Wear your respirator and rubber gloves while spraying dye. Mist the dye solution across the fabric. For deep color, apply the dye in several thin coats. Avoid soaking the fabric. If you apply too much dye solution, it may liquefy the resist. You can also apply dye solution with a foam brush, but be very careful not to soak the fabric.

10. Cover the damp, dye-coated fabric with a piece of plastic sheeting. If you must move the fabric while it is batching, roll it carefully in the plastic. Keep the fabric at room temperature (70° or more) for at least 24 hours.

11. Rinse excess dye from the fabric, then wash in warm water with a mild detergent or Synthrapol. If desired, air-dry the fabric after batching for 24 hours, and rinse and wash later. Waiting several days will not hurt the fabric and may actually help set the color.

12. Hang the fabric to dry or dry it in the dryer.

13. Clean your tools with running water.

Baby Bolero by Sarah Kalvin and Jane Dunnewold, 1995, San Antonio, Texas. Hand-painted cotton velveteen. (Original pattern by Sarah Kalvin)

For Inspiration

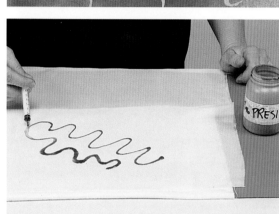

Hand Painting

Use your imagination! Paint whole areas of cloth or paint a checkerboard. Apply the resist with a syringe, a foam brush, or use a small bristle brush and draw fine lines. Remember scale. A large brush is great for broad strokes. For more delicate lines, use a smaller, tapered brush.

Materials

Slightly padded work surface

Plastic drop cloth or sheeting

Respirator

Rubber gloves

Fabric (prewashed, dried, and ironed)

Shallow container

½ to 1 cup water-based resist

Foam and bristle brushes or syringe

Paper towels

Dye Solution (recipe on page 53)

PreVal Sprayer or plant mister

Mild detergent or Synthrapol

Procedure

1. Assemble your materials and prepare your work area.

2. Stretch out the dry, ironed fabric on the work surface.

3. Pour the resist into a shallow container.

4. Use a brush or syringe to pattern your fabric. Fill the syringe by inserting the tip in the resist and slowly pulling out the plunger. Gently push the plunger while moving the syringe across the fabric. Flowing motions are easiest at the start. Use a paper towel to catch drips. Use the bristle brush to make dots, swirls, and other embellishments.

5. Lift a corner of the fabric to see if the resist penetrated through the fabric. If the resist sits only on the front of the fabric, it will not adequately block the dye. If necessary, reapply resist until the pattern shows on the back. Allow to dry for 24 hours.

6. Clean your tools. Pour any unused resist back into the bottle.

7. Mix the dye solution. If desired, thicken the dye with sodium alginate. Thick dye residue readily washes away when the resist is rinsed out.

8. Fill the PreVal Sprayer or plant mister with dye solution. (If you thicken the dye, use a foam brush to apply it.)

9. Wear your respirator and rubber gloves while spraying dye. Mist the dye solution across the fabric. For deep color, apply the dye in several thin coats. Avoid soaking the fabric. If you apply too much dye solution, it may liquefy the resist. You can also apply dye solution with a foam brush, but be very careful not to soak the fabric.

10. Cover the damp, dye-coated fabric with a piece of plastic sheeting. If you must move the fabric while it is batching, roll it carefully in the plastic. Keep the fabric at room temperature (70° or more) for at least 24 hours.

11. Rinse excess dye from the fabric, then wash in warm water with a mild detergent or Synthrapol. If desired, air-dry the fabric after batching for 24 hours and rinse and wash later. Waiting several days will not hurt the fabric and may actually help set the color.

12. Hang the fabric to dry or dry it in the dryer.

13. Clean your tools with running water.

For inspiration

*Untitled **Kimono** by Agnes Welsh Eyster, 1995, San Antonio, Texas. Dyed and overdyed cottons. Silk-screened, collaged, and machine embroidered.*

Using Water-Based Resists with Bleach

Discharging dark fabric that has been treated with a water-based resist provides interesting depth, color, and pattern. If you intend to experiment with resists and the discharging process, remember that silk and wool may be damaged by bleach. For best results, use cotton or rayon. For more information on working with bleach, refer to "Bleach Discharge" on pages 63–73.

Because you will be spraying bleach, work outside if possible. Use a box fan to increase ventilation, wear a respirator and rubber gloves, and protect the area surrounding your work surface with plastic sheeting. If you are using a quarter- or half-face respirator, wear protective goggles.

Magic Nights by Shelly Kyle, 1994, San Antonio, Texas. Discharged black cotton velveteen. Hand painted with permanent markers.

. . . . For Inspiration . . . . .

Stamping

See "Stamping Basics" on pages 20–27.

Materials

Box fan
Slightly padded work surface
Plastic drop cloth or sheeting
Respirator
Rubber gloves
Fabric (prewashed, dried, and ironed)

Shallow container for resist
½ to 1 cup water-based resist
Foam brushes
Hand-cut or commercial stamps
Household bleach
PreVal Sprayer or plant mister

Procedure

1. Assemble your materials and prepare your work area.
2. Stretch out the dry, ironed fabric on the work surface.
3. Fill your washing machine with cool water and set the controls so the machine will not cycle. You want it to be ready when you complete the discharge process.
4. Pour the resist into a shallow container.
5. Apply the resist to your stamp using a foam brush. Brush enough resist onto the stamp to moisten it, but not so much that it drips. You need enough resist to penetrate the fabric, but not so much that you can't make a clear image.

6. Press the stamp on the fabric. Lift a corner of the fabric to see if the resist penetrated. If the resist sits only on the front of the fabric, it will not adequately block the bleach. If necessary, reapply resist until the pattern shows on the back. Allow to dry for 24 hours.
7. Clean your tools. Pour any unused resist back into the bottle.
8. Fill the PreVal Sprayer or plant mister with household bleach.
9. Wear your respirator, protective goggles, and rubber gloves while spraying bleach. Spray the bleach in a sweeping motion, covering the fabric with an even coat. Avoid soaking the fabric; it may liquefy the resist. The discharging action will be immediate.

10. Carefully transfer the fabric to the washing machine and begin the wash cycle.
11. Hang the fabric to dry or dry it in the dryer.
12. Clean your tools with running water to remove all traces of bleach. Pour any unused bleach back into the bottle.

Stenciling

See "Stenciling Basics" on pages 28–31.

Materials

Box fan

Slightly padded work surface

Plastic drop cloth or sheeting

Respirator

Rubber gloves

Fabric (prewashed, dried, and ironed)

Shallow container for resist

½ to 1 cup water-based resist

Foam brushes

Hand-cut or commercial stencils

Household bleach

PreVal Sprayer or plant mister

Optional Materials

Spray adhesive

Procedure

1. Assemble your materials and prepare your work area.
2. Stretch out the dry, ironed fabric on the work surface.
3. Fill your washing machine with cool water and set the controls so the machine will not cycle. You want it to be ready when you complete the discharge process.
4. You may want to lightly spray the back of the stencil with spray adhesive. This helps the stencil stick to your fabric and makes your job easier. Carefully place the stencil on the fabric.
5. Pour the resist into a shallow container.
6. Dampen a foam brush with resist. Carefully apply the resist to open areas of the stencil. Try to saturate the open areas completely with resist. Lift a corner of the fabric to see if the resist penetrated through the fabric. If the resist sits only on the front of the fabric, it will not adequately block the bleach. If necessary, reapply resist until the pattern shows on the back. Allow to dry for 24 hours.
7. Clean your tools. Pour any unused resist back into the bottle.
8. Fill the PreVal Sprayer or plant mister with household bleach.
9. Wear your respirator, protective goggles, and rubber gloves while spraying bleach. Spray the bleach in a sweeping motion, covering the fabric with an even coat. Avoid soaking the fabric; it may liquefy the resist. The discharging action will be immediate.
10. Carefully transfer the fabric to the washing machine and begin the wash cycle.
11. Hang the fabric to dry or dry it in the dryer.
12. Clean your tools with running water to remove all traces of bleach. Pour any unused bleach back into the bottle.

Hand Painting

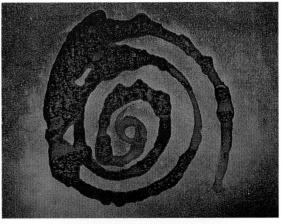

Materials

Box fan
Slightly padded work surface
Plastic drop cloth or sheeting
  Respirator
Rubber gloves
Fabric (prewashed, dried,
  and ironed)

Shallow container for resist
½ to 1 cup water-based resist
Foam and bristle brushes or syringe
Paper towels
Household bleach
PreVal Sprayer or plant mister

Procedure

1. Assemble your materials and prepare your work area.
2. Stretch out the dry, ironed fabric on the work surface.
3. Fill your washing machine with cool water and set the controls so the machine will not cycle. You want it to be ready when you complete the discharge process.
4. Pour ½ to 1 cup of resist into a shallow container.
5. Use a brush or syringe to pattern your fabric. Fill the syringe by inserting the tip in the resist and slowly pulling out the plunger. Gently push the plunger while moving the syringe across the fabric. Flowing motions are easiest at the start. Use a paper towel to catch drips. Use the bristle brush to make dots, swirls, and other embellishments.

6. Lift a corner of the fabric to see if the resist penetrated through the fabric. If the resist sits only on the front of the fabric, it will not adequately block the bleach. If necessary, reapply resist until the pattern shows on the back. Allow to dry for 24 hours.
7. Clean your tools. Pour any unused resist back into the bottle.
8. Fill the PreVal Sprayer or plant mister with household bleach.
9. Wear your respirator, protective goggles, and rubber gloves while spraying bleach. Spray the bleach in a sweeping motion, covering the fabric with an even coat. Avoid soaking the fabric; it may liquefy the resist. The discharging action will be immediate.
10. Carefully transfer the fabric to the washing machine and begin the wash cycle.
11. Hang the fabric to dry or dry it in the dryer.
12. Clean your tools with running water to remove all traces of bleach. Pour any unused bleach back into the bottle.

Using Water-Based Resists with Fabric Paints

Stamping

See "Stamping Basics" on pages 20–27.

Materials

Slightly padded work surface	½ to 1 cup water-based resist
Plastic drop cloth or sheeting	Foam brushes
Respirator	Hand-cut or commercial stamps
Rubber gloves	Fabric paints (thinned or premixed
Fabric (prewashed, dried,	watercolor formula)
and ironed)	Stir stick
Shallow containers for resist and	PreVal Sprayer or plant mister
for thinning paint	Mild detergent

Procedure

1. Assemble your materials and prepare your work area.

2. Stretch out the dry, ironed fabric on the work surface.

3. Pour the resist into a shallow container.

4. Apply the resist to your stamp using a foam brush. Brush enough resist onto the stamp to moisten it, but not so much that it drips. You need enough resist to penetrate the fabric, but not so much that you can't make a clear image.

5. Press the resist-coated stamp firmly on your fabric. After stamping, lift a corner of the fabric to see if the resist penetrated through the fabric. If the resist sits only on the front of the fabric, it will not adequately block the paint. If necessary, reapply resist until the stamp impression shows on the back. Allow to dry for 24 hours.

6. Clean your tools. Pour any unused resist back into the bottle.

7. If necessary, use water to thin the fabric paint to the consistency of milk. Fill the PreVal Sprayer or plant mister with paint.

8. Wear your respirator and rubber gloves while spraying fabric paint. Mist the paint across the surface of the cloth. For a deep color, apply the paint in several thin coats. Avoid soaking the fabric; it may liquefy the resist. You can also apply paint with a foam brush, but be very careful not to soak the fabric.

9. Allow the paint to dry for 24 hours. Follow the manufacturer's instructions for setting the paints. This generally entails ironing at high heat for several minutes. Iron the wrong side of your fabric so the resist does not stick to your iron.

10. After you have set the paint, wash the fabric in the washing machine. Use warm water and a mild detergent.

11. Hang the fabric to dry or dry it in the dryer.

12. Clean your tools with running water.

Stenciling

See "Stenciling Basics" on pages 28–31.

Materials

Slightly padded work surface

Plastic drop cloth or sheeting

Respirator

Rubber gloves

Fabric (prewashed, dried, and ironed)

Shallow containers for resist and for thinning paint

½ to 1 cup water-based resist

Foam brushes

Hand-cut or commercial stencils

Fabric paints (thinned or premixed watercolor formula)

Stir stick

PreVal Sprayer or plant mister

Mild detergent

Optional Materials

Spray adhesive

Procedure

1. Assemble your materials and prepare your work area.

2. Stretch out the dry, ironed fabric on the work surface.

3. You may want to lightly spray the back of the stencil with spray adhesive. This helps the stencil stick to your fabric and makes your job easier. Carefully place the stencil on the fabric.

4. Pour the resist into a shallow container.

5. Coat a foam brush with resist. Carefully apply the resist to open areas of the stencil. Saturate the open areas completely with resist. Lift a corner of the fabric to see if the resist penetrated through the fabric. If the resist sits only on the front of the fabric, it will not adequately block the paint. If necessary, reapply resist until the pattern shows on the back. Allow to dry for 24 hours.

6. Clean your tools. Pour any unused resist back into the bottle.

7. If necessary, use water to thin fabric paint to the consistency of milk. Fill the PreVal Sprayer or plant mister with paint.

8. Wear your respirator and rubber gloves while spraying fabric paint. Mist the paint across the surface of the cloth. For a deep color, apply the paint in several thin coats. Avoid soaking the fabric; it may liquefy the resist. You can also apply paint with a foam brush, but be very careful not to soak the fabric.

9. Allow the paint to dry for 24 hours. Follow the manufacturer's instructions for setting the paints. This generally entails ironing at high heat for several minutes. Iron the wrong side of your fabric so the resist does not stick to your iron.

10. After you have set the paint, wash the fabric in the washing machine. Use warm water and a mild detergent.

11. Hang the fabric to dry or dry it in the dryer.

12. Clean your tools with running water.

Hand Painting

Materials

Slightly padded work surface
Plastic drop cloth or sheeting
Respirator
Rubber gloves
Fabric (prewashed, dried,
  and ironed)
Shallow containers for resist and
  for thinning paint

½ to 1 cup water-based resist
Foam and bristle brushes or syringe
Paper towels
Fabric paints (thinned or premixed
  watercolor formula)
Stir stick
PreVal Sprayer or plant mister
Mild detergent

Procedure

1. Assemble your materials and prepare your work area.

2. Stretch out the dry, ironed fabric on the work surface.

3. Pour the resist into a shallow container.

4. Use a brush or syringe to pattern your fabric. Fill the syringe by inserting the tip in the resist and slowly pulling out the plunger. Gently push the plunger while moving the syringe across the fabric. Flowing motions are easiest at the start. Use a paper towel to catch drips. Use the bristle brush to make dots, swirls, and other embellishments.

5. Lift a corner of the fabric to see if the resist penetrated through the fabric. If the resist sits only on the front of the fabric, it will not adequately block the paint. If necessary, reapply resist until the pattern shows on the back. Allow to dry for 24 hours.

6. Clean your tools. Pour any unused resist back into the bottle.

7. If necessary, use water to thin fabric paint to the consistency of milk. Fill the PreVal Sprayer or plant mister with paint.

8. Wear your respirator and rubber gloves while spraying fabric paint. Mist the paint across the surface of the cloth. For a deep color, apply the paint in several thin coats. Avoid soaking the fabric; it may liquefy the resist. You can also apply paint with a foam brush, but be very careful not to soak the fabric.

9. Allow the paint to dry for 24 hours. Follow the manufacturer's instructions for setting the paints. This generally entails ironing at high heat for several minutes. Iron the wrong side of your fabric so the resist does not stick to your iron.

10. After you have set the paint, wash the fabric in the washing machine. Use warm water and a mild detergent.

11. Hang the fabric to dry or dry it in the dryer.

Tips and Variations
for Working with Water-Based Resists

❖ Try layering more than one application of color or resist before washing the cloth. For instance, stencil on the resist using one pattern. Spray the cloth with thinned fabric paint. Dry and heat-set. Then apply a second layer of resist in the same pattern, overlapping the previous pattern if desired. Apply a second, compatible color. Heat-set, then wash out. Multiple layers!

❖ Apply a heavy coat of potato-starch resist or Inko resist paste with a foam brush. When the resist dries, crush the fabric. Mist the surface with dye, paint, or bleach. The result will be a fine-lined, crackly pattern, much like batik.

❖ Apply resist to dark fabric and discharge. Wash the fabric, then apply a second layer of resist. Mist with dye solution or paint. Batch or heat-set and wash. This basic formula can be repeated a number of times for an increasingly complex surface.

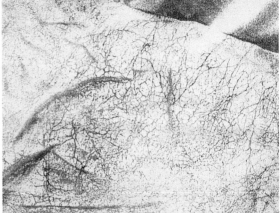

Foils and Glitters

Metallic foils and glitters add depth and brilliance to dyed and painted fabric. Each product provides heady results, and each has minor drawbacks. Base your choices on the look you want for your complex cloth.

Metallic foils are thin layers of metallic plastic fused to a sheet of cellophane. You apply either a liquid glue or fusible web to fabric, then iron the metallic foil to the adhesive. When the foil has cooled, you peel away the cellophane. Foils are bright and will not tarnish over time. You can wash cloth embellished with metallic foil by hand or machine (gentle cycle). If you want to use metallic foil in a project that will need to be dry-cleaned, have a sample tested before you make the project. Dry-cleaning chemicals can strip color from the foil (much like it does from sequins).

Glitter is a versatile product. Use it to provide hints of sparkle across the surface of a cloth or to create concentrated areas of brilliance. Glitter is packaged in four forms. You can purchase it loose, ranging from microfine powder to larger cut shapes (such as hearts or geometrics); mixed into a paint base; as a glitter stick (similar to a gluestick); and in a spray. Glitter sprays have a clear base that binds the glitter to the fabric.

Glitter products are stable and can be washed and dry-cleaned safely. Their glimmery highlights may be just the touch a length of cloth needs to boost its appeal and make it special.

Metallic Foils

Metallic foils are often sold in craft stores with related items (such as glues, binders, sealants, and gemstones). The company marketing this metallic-foil "system" had a particular kind of craft project in mind. You may not need the entire system to create complex cloth. By experimenting with foils, fabric glues, and fusible webs, I have found that certain brands provide more reliable results than others. The products I describe here provide good results. (You can order these products from the suppliers on page 156.)

If you decide to experiment with other products, make samples. Some brands of foil are lighter weight than others and melt when touched with an iron. (Use a pressing cloth!) I ruined a silk screen by using a fabric glue I could not remove. Many of these products are relatively new and are still being perfected. Don't give up if your results are disappointing. Go back to the products I've suggested here,

Once again, the weave of the fabric is an important consideration. Foils adhere to heavy- as well as lightweight weaves, but the texture affects the way the foil looks. For best results, make a sample to test how the foil will look on your fabric. Silk-screened glue generally provides better coverage on a textured surface than stamping, stenciling, or using a fusible web. Smooth, evenly woven fabric works beautifully with any of the applications.

Metallic foils are best applied as one of the last complex-cloth processes. Foils, which are nonabsorbent, cannot be safely immersed in dye for lengths of time, and many fabric paints do not adequately cover foils.

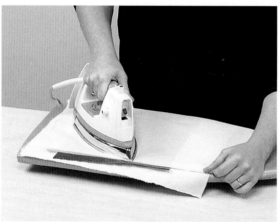

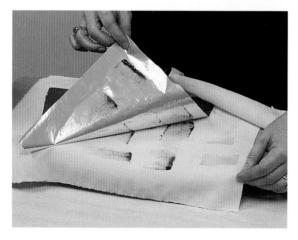

Metallic Foil Recipes

Applying Metallic Foil with Glue

Materials

Fabric (prewashed, dried, ironed)
Aleene's Stretchable, Flexible
   Fabric Glue or Elmer's Fabric Glue
Shallow container for glue
Foam and bristle brushes in
   several widths

Iron and ironing board
Craft scissors
Iron-on metallic foil
Pressing cloth

Optional Materials

Extension cord

Procedure

1. Assemble your materials and prepare your work area.

2. Stretch out the dry, ironed fabric on the work surface.

3. Pour a small amount of glue into a shallow container. Dip a foam or bristle brush in the glue. A big brush works well for broad strokes. A small brush works well for detailed patterns. For free-form patterns and lines, try squeezing the glue directly from the bottle.

4. Paint a design on your fabric. Make broad brush strokes or fine lines, dots, and squiggles. The more glue you apply, the more consistent the coverage.

5. Wait for the glue to completely dry. (It will look clear.) While the glue is drying, wash your tools with warm water and a soft brush. When this glue dries, it is permanent. Dried glue will ruin brushes, silk screens, and stencils.

6. Turn the iron to the cotton (high) setting. Steam is not necessary.

7. Cut a piece of foil large enough to cover the area where you painted the glue. If the foil is not large enough to cover the entire surface, lay more than one piece over the design, matching up the edges. *Always position the foil color side up.* You must be able to see the foil color. (The cellophane layer is on top.) If you turn the foil color side down, with the back of it facing you, it will not adhere. Check this first if you are having problems getting the foil to stick.

8. Cover the foil with a pressing cloth. Iron over the foil/glue surface, applying as much pressure as possible with the iron.

9. Remove the pressing cloth and peel away a corner of the cellophane. When you peel away the cellophane, you should leave a solid foil image on the fabric. If the foil did not cover the glue completely, you can reposition the foil and iron more foil onto the surface.

10. If you are working on a long piece of fabric, reposition the foil and continue ironing.

Troubleshooting

There are three possible causes for poor coverage. First, you may not have used enough glue. The more glue you apply, the more consistent the coverage. Or, you may not have used enough pressure when you ironed the metallic foil onto the glue. Reposition the foil and try again. Lastly, it may be the kind of foil you are using. Metallic foils available through office-supply stores may need to cool before you peel away the cellophane. Experiment with ironing the foil, letting it cool, then peeling away the cellophane.

Tips and Variations
for Working with Metallic Foils and Glue

- ❖ **Stamping**: Follow the instructions for stamping fabric paint (pages 78–79). Spread the glue on a stamp, using a foam brush. Stamp the glue onto the fabric. Wait for the glue to dry, then apply the metallic foil as described above.

    The stamping action leaves a very thin layer of glue on the fabric. This results in a faint foiled image. If you want a heavier image, try stenciling or silk screening.

- ❖ **Stenciling:** Follow the instructions for stenciling fabric paint (pages 80–81). Wait for the glue to dry, then apply metallic foil as described above.

    Stenciling allows you to control the amount of glue applied to the surface of the fabric, ensuring better coverage than stamping.

- ❖ **Silk screening:** Follow the instructions for silk screening fabric paint (pages 82–85). Wait for the glue to dry, then apply metallic foil as described above.

    Silk screening gives you more control over the amount of glue applied than any other technique. Coverage is smooth and complete. This means that the ironed-on foil surface will also be smooth and complete. If your primary concern is coverage, use silk screening.

    Always clean the silk screen immediately after you finish screening. Glue dries quickly and can ruin the mesh.

- ❖ Consider ironing several colors of metallic foils together. Foil sticks to itself. This makes it easy to lay down one color, iron it to the glue, then iron the second foil on top of the first. The result will be a two-colored image, varied enough to add interest and dimension.

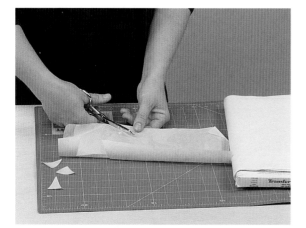

Applying Metallic Foil with Fusible Web

Fusible web is intended for use in a variety of craft and sewing applications. The fusible web—a heat-activated glue in sheet form—is usually bonded to a paper backing. Each product differs slightly from the others; read the manufacturer's instructions prior to use.

Transfer Fusing™, Stitch Witchery®, and Wonder-Under® are just a few brands of fusible-web products. Transfer Fusing and Wonder-Under provide a dense and effective bond. Stitch Witchery provides a much lighter, more weblike bond.

The advantage of using fusible web is you can draw on the paper backing, then use the drawing as a cutting guide. You can also fold the fusible web and cut paper dolls or snowflakes.

Choose fusible webs based on whether you want complete coverage or a more open appearance.

Materials

Fabric (prewashed, dried, and ironed)
Iron and ironing board
Fusible web

Craft scissors
Iron-on metallic foil
Pressing cloth

Optional Materials

Extension cord

Slightly padded work surface

Procedure

1. Assemble your materials and prepare your work area.

2. Stretch out the dry, ironed fabric on your ironing board or padded work surface. Turn the iron to the cotton (high) setting. Steam is not necessary.

3. Cut shapes from the fusible web.

4. Position a fusible-web shape on the fabric. The shiny, glue side of the fusible web should be against the fabric.

5. Iron over the shape. It takes only a second or two for the fusible web to melt.

6. Gently peel away the paper backing while the fusible web is still hot. If you have trouble peeling away the paper, reheat the fusible web with the iron. The only thing left on the cloth should be the faintly shiny fusible-web image.

7. Cut a piece of foil large enough to cover the fusible-web shape. *Always position the foil color side up.* You must be able to see the foil color. (The cellophane layer is on top.) If you turn the foil color side down, with the back facing you, it will not adhere. Check this first if you are having problems getting the foil to stick.

There are two ways to approach multiple fusible-web shapes. You can iron all the shapes, then return to apply the foil, or you can apply a fusible-web shape, iron the foil, then proceed to the next shape. Your working style will depend on the length of your fabric, the size of your work space, and the complexity of the design.

8. Cover the foil with a pressing cloth. Iron over the shape, applying moderate pressure. Count to 10 as you iron the shape.

9. Remove the pressing cloth and peel up a corner of the cellophane. When you peel away the cellophane, you should leave a solid foil image on the fabric. If the foil did not cover the glue completely, you can reposition it and iron more foil onto the surface.

10. If you are working on a long piece of fabric, reposition the foil and continue ironing.

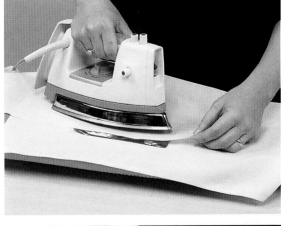

Save partially used foil. It can be reused until all the foil is gone and only clear cellophane remains.

Troubleshooting

There are three possible causes for poor coverage. First, the iron may not have been hot enough. Make sure the iron is on the cotton (high) setting, and count to 10 as you press the foil onto the fusible web. Or, the texture of the fabric may have kept the fusible web from bonding completely to the surface. A heavier weave is harder to cover using this process than a smooth weave. Cut a new piece of fusible web and try again. This time, press hard to ensure contact between fusible web and cloth. The fusible web may not reheat well. Allow the foil/fusible web to cool before you peel away the cellophane. Finally, if that doesn't help, switch to another fusible-web product.

Glitter Recipes

You can hardly go wrong with glitter. Easy to apply, it is the icing on the cake of your complex-cloth design. This section provides an overview of the many different ways to apply glitter.

Applying Loose Glitter

Materials

Fabric (prewashed, dried, and ironed)
Assorted fabric paints

Assorted colors and cuts of glitter powder (microfine to large)
Plastic spoon

Procedure

1. Using any of the techniques discussed in this book, apply fabric paint to your fabric. (Never mix glitter into a paint you intend to silk-screen; it may clog the screen, and the mesh will be impossible to clean.)
2. Scatter loose glitter across the wet paint. Shake a spoonful of loose glitter from several feel above the piece for an allover, lightly glittered look. Sprinkle a spoonful of glitter directly over an image for a more concentrated glitter application. The paint will bind the glitter permanently.
3. Always take your fabric outdoors before you shake off excess glitter. Glitter—especially the microfine stuff—is nearly impossible to remove from carpets, clothing, and hair.

Applying Glitter Paint

Packaged in tubes and squeeze bottles, glitter paints are ideal for drawing fine lines and highlighting large painted areas. Most glitter-paint bases are transparent, making it easy to blend the glitter base into whatever color is painted underneath. When dry, the faint base-color paint is very subtle, allowing the glitter to shine.

Materials

Fabric (prewashed, dried, and ironed)

Assorted glitter paints

Procedure

Use glitter paints as you would fabric paints in every application technique except silk screening. Even microfine glitter is too large to pass through a silk-screen mesh.

Using a Glitter Stick

Glitter sticks are available in a wide range of colors. The base is clear and permanent when dried and heat-set. These are magical tools—wherever you draw with the stick, you leave a trail of fine glitter behind. One note of caution: the base may yellow over time. This is especially noticeable on white fabric. To be on the safe side, use glitter sticks with colored fabric only.

Materials

Fabric (prewashed, dried, and ironed)

Delta/Slomons® Glitter Sticks

Procedure

Use glitter sticks as you would gluesticks, rubbing the stick across the fabric. When the glue is dry to the touch, use an iron (cotton or high setting, no steam) to heat-set the glitter and glue.

Balinese Theater Coat by Renita Kuhn and Jane Dunnewold, 1993, San Antonio, Texas. Dyed and overdyed silks and rayons. Painted, silk-screened, foiled, and embellished with machine embroidery and beads.

For Inspiration

Glitter Spray

Glitter sprays are made by combining a microfine glitter with a base that is permanent when dry.

Materials

Fabric (prewashed, dried, and ironed)

Glitter spray

Procedure

1. Spray glitter across the fabric, holding the can 8" to 10" away.

2. Allow the glitter spray to dry. Apply a second coat if desired.

3. Like glitter sticks, glitter spray must be heat-set. When the spray is dry to the touch, use an iron (cotton or high setting, no steam) to heat-set the glitter.

Tips and Variations for Working with Glitter

❖ Mix microfine glitter into a fabric paint you intend to stencil. The glitter caught under the surface of the paint will add depth to the overall appearance of the cloth. This technique is most successful when used with stenciling or freehand painting.

❖ Sprinkle loose glitter over damp puff paint. When the puff paint dries and puffs, the glitter will be imbedded in the paint.

❖ Use glitter paint to set up a background for additional painting. Squeeze paint onto your fabric, then spread it with a foam brush. The paint base will be very pale when dry, and the glitter will be distributed across the cloth. Stamping or silk screening on this surface with a transparent fabric paint will allow for a great deal of layering—and the glitter will show through the transparent layers.

❖ Complete a complex cloth and sew it into a garment. Spray the finished garment with glitter spray, then heat-set. You will sparkle!

Flight to India by Renita Kuhn and Jane Dunnewold, 1994, San Antonio, Texas. Silk-screened and stamped white cotton and silk. Foiled, puff-painted, and beaded. (Original design by Renita Kuhn)

Untitled Vest by Jane Dunnewold, 1991, San Antonio, Texas. Stamped silk noil. Embroidered and beaded.

For inspiration

Baby Quilt *by Jane Dunnewold, 1995, San Antonio, Texas. 30" x 36". Solvent transfers on silk.*
Foiled, beaded, and machine quilted. (Photo by Jane Dunnewold)

Photocopy Transfers

No matter which transfer process or combination of processes you choose, photocopy transfers will expand your repertoire, allowing you to incorporate imagery into your work that you might not otherwise use. The photocopy machine is a wonderful tool for those of us who lack drawing skills. A wide selection of noncopyrighted material is available through bookstores and libraries. Once you find the image you had in mind, you can change it any number of ways—cut it apart, copy it and draw on the copy, or enlarge or reduce it.

The photocopy processes in this book include solvent transfers, iron-on transfers, transfers using Bondex™ Mending Tape, and transfers using gel medium. The first process uses a solvent to transfer images to cloth. The second process uses a special paper to transfer color pictures to cloth. (This requires a copy shop with a color copier.) The third process uses Bondex Mending Tape to transfer black-and-white images to fabric.

The fourth transfer process uses gel medium to bind the ink of a photocopy to the fabric surface. Gel medium affects the hand of the fabric, making it considerably stiffer.

When you select fabric for use with photocopy processes, choose a smooth, even weave. Medium-weight silk habotai, rayon broadcloth, and pima cotton are great choices for photocopy techniques. In general, the more textured or loosely woven the cloth, the more fractured the final print. Avoid nylon and knit fabrics. Solvents may destroy the nylon, and the stretchiness of a knit makes it hard to get a clear impression.

Remember that photocopies, even color copies, are transparent. No matter which application process you use, you will be able to see the background color of the fabric . Most of the time, a lighter background is better than a darker background. If the background is any color other than white, it will alter the colors of the iron-on transfer. If in doubt, do a sample before beginning your work.

Art and Copyright

There is a great deal of discussion concerning the use of "appropriated" imagery—that is, incorporating pictures and words created by someone else into your work. When material has a copyright, it is against the law to use it without permission. Most of us have heard of legal battles waged against individuals or businesses who have used well-known characters or symbols to advertise products without permission. Yet many prominent artists have used someone else's drawings or photographs, or even cartoon characters, in one-of-a-kind art collages shown in museums around the world. The issue can be very confusing.

I have mentioned Dover Publications, which provides wonderful, copyright-free books on all kinds of subjects. (See "Bibliography" on page 155.) Libraries and bookstores carry these as well as other sources of copyright-free material. I encourage you to use these resources. If you find another source you would like to use, let your conscience be your guide, but you may want to write for permission. One-time use on a piece of fabric you are making for yourself is very different from mass production of yardage with the intent to make a financial profit.

Fullness of Life by Jane Dunnewold, 1992, San Antonio, Texas, 32" x 17" x 2". Discharged and painted fabrics. Solvent transfer on silk. Foiled, beaded, and embroidered. (Photo by Jane Dunnewold)

Safety Precautions

As with any of the processes discussed in this book, use appropriate safety precautions. Solvents contain a range of chemicals. These chemicals, if inhaled as fumes or absorbed through the skin, are potentially hazardous to your health. Wear rubber gloves and work outside if you can. If you must work inside, set up a fan and wear a respirator and rubber gloves. If you are using a quarter- or half-face respirator, wear protective goggles when spraying solvents. *If you are considering pregnancy, are pregnant, or are nursing, do not work with solvents.*

A variety of techniques are offered here, so it is possible to work with photocopy transfers no matter what your safety concerns.

Unlike a dust mask, which keeps fine particles out of your nose and mouth, a respirator contains cartridges that clean the air as you breathe through the mask. Respirators are not expensive and are an important safety precaution for working with solvents.

Photocopy Transfer Recipes

Photocopy Transfers Using a Solvent

Transferring a photocopy using a solvent is very simple. You apply solvent to a photocopy (this liquefies the ink), place the photocopy on the fabric, then rub the damp surface vigorously to transfer the ink. Solvent transfers are permanent, washable, and dry cleanable, and they provide instant gratification.

Printmakers have long used solvents to transfer images from newspapers and other sources to artwork in progress. We seem to have a fascination with transfers like these, perhaps because they are so immediate.

I experimented with a number of solvents while learning how to transfer photocopies. I didn't have much luck with any of them and was about to throw out the whole idea when I discovered Dupont™ 3661S Automotive Lacquer Thinner. Readily available and easy to use, the images transferred using this solvent are crystal clear and do not bleed. I was ecstatic!

I recommend this product because it works so well. If you cannot find it or have access to other products, you may want to experiment. Solvents transfer most black-and-white photocopies, but some copiers use a toner system that is not affected by solvent. If this happens, you'll know it, because the ink will not liquefy. In the beginning, it is a good idea to make black-and-white copies on more than one copier. Then you can experiment and know immediately which copiers you used are compatible with the process. Ironically, if your copy is too high quality, you may get a poor transfer. Laser copies will not work at all, because the inking system on a laser printer is different from the toner system on a photocopier.

In experimenting with a safer alternative to automotive lacquer thinner, I've found that Citrisolve, a cleaning product, transfers black-and-white photocopies safely and effectively. You can substitute Citrisolve in this recipe if desired. It is slightly greasier than the automotive lacquer thinner and smears easily while damp. See "Resources" on page 156.

The black on your copy should be very dark. This is an indication that the toner was working properly when you made the copy. High-contrast copies—obvious positive and negative space—make the best transfers while you are learning. Too much gray—like backgrounds—can turn into a mess if you apply too much solvent. Black-and-white line drawings are ideal for first attempts.

You can also transfer color copies. The process is essentially the same, but because color copies are printed on higher-quality paper than most black-and-white copies, it may take more solvent to wet the image enough to transfer it. Color copies are printed using a four-color ink system. The colors are layered as they are printed. This can mean an uneven coloration when the transfer is made. Skin tones in photographs frequently turn red or yellow and look garish. If you want to experiment with a color image, start with something other than a family protrait.

To include letters or words, make a transparency of your photocopy before making copies to use as transfers. Without the transparency, the writing would be transferred to the fabric backwards.

Many copiers have the ability to enlarge or reduce. Use this as part of your creative process when you plan your design.

Silks do particularly well with solvent transfers, and silk habotai is my all-around favorite. It produces crisp images, and the fabric is so thin the image penetrates the cloth completely. This is especially useful if you want legible lettering. Just print on the wrong side of the fabric instead of copying the letters to a transparency.

Use a PreVal Sprayer rather than a plant mister when working with Dupont 3661S Automotive Lacquer Thinner because the plant mister drips too much.

Materials

Box fan
Respirator
Rubber gloves
1 yd. muslin or other
  smooth-weave fabric
PreVal Sprayer

Dupont 3661S Automotive
  Lacquer Thinner
Fabric (prewashed, dried,
  and ironed)
Black-and-white or color photocopy
Old plastic or wooden spoon

Optional Materials

Shallow glass dish

Block of Fun Foam (see page 21)

Procedure

1. Assemble your materials and prepare your work area. Cover your work table with 2 or 3 layers of folded muslin so you have a slightly padded surface. The muslin absorbs any excess solvent and keeps the image from blurring.

2. Fill the PreVal Sprayer with the solvent.

3. Stretch out the dry, ironed fabric on your muslin-covered work surface.

4. Place the photocopy on the fabric, ink side down.

5. Wear your respirator and rubber gloves when spraying solvent. Mist the back of the copy with solvent. Keep the bottle as straight as possible. The sprayer will leak if tilted at too great an angle.

Mist the back side of the copy until you can see the image on the front through the back. This is the most challenging part of the process. Too much spray will blur the ink; too little will result in an incomplete transfer. It takes practice to spray just enough solvent on the paper to transfer the image clearly and completely. If you don't get enough the first time, keep trying.

If you are transferring a color copy, you may need to spray the image more than you would if it were black and white. Spraying the front of a color copy may make the transfer easier to complete.

6. Holding the copy in place with one gloved hand, carefully rub the back of the paper with the spoon. Hold the paper firmly in place, or the image will smear. This is not a delicate procedure! Press down on the spoon and rub firmly to transfer the image.

7. Carefully lift one edge of the copy to check your progress. *Do not remove the paper entirely.* It is very difficult to reposition the copy if the image needs more work. Peeling up one corner will show you where you need to spray again.

8. When the transfer is complete, dispose of the copy. It cannot be reused. No heat setting is needed.

9. Pour any unused solvent back into the can. Wash your tools with soap and water.

Optional Procedure

One of my gifted students, Shelly Kyle, came up with another method for transferring photocopies without using the PreVal Sprayer. Try this if you do not want to use a sprayer or to compare techniques.

1. Prepare your work surface and fabric as described in steps 1–4.

2. Pour a small amount of solvent into a glass dish. You must use glass; plastic or foam containers will melt.

3. Dip a corner of the Fun Foam block into the solvent.

4. Rub the back of the photocopy with the dampened block. The image should transfer easily. If the transfer is incomplete, dip the block into the solvent and rub the copy again until the image transfers.

5. Pour any unused solvent back into the can. Wash the block with soap and water.

Tips and Variations

for Transferring Photocopies Using a Solvent

❖ Make a collage on the surface of the fabric by applying one transfer, waiting for it to dry, then applying additional transfers, one at a time. As long as you do not saturate the cloth, the first images will not blur.

❖ You can also make a collage by cutting and pasting photocopies until you get a design you like. Photocopy the paste-up and use it as the final transfer.

❖ Hand color transfers with thinned-down fabric paint. Put a dime-size drop of paint on a palette or plastic tray and add enough water to make it slightly runny. Or, use a watercolor-type paint like Deka Silk. Scale the brush to the size of the picture you are painting. Keep the brush fairly dry so the paint doesn't bleed outside the edges of the image. Start by touching the brush to the inner area of a shape. The paint will then bleed up close to the edge of the image, without going beyond it. Proceed in this manner, painting inside the lines and allowing the paint to bleed close to the edges. I prefer a painted image that does not obscure but enhances the photocopy transfer. You may prefer to use a heavier paint so the original drawing/transfer is not so apparent. This is a matter of personal preference.

❖ You can also enhance transfers using colored pencils or fabric crayons and markers. Test for permanence if it will make a difference to your final project!

❖ Shelly Kyle uses her transfer process to make terrific rubber stamps on Fun Foam. Instead of transferring the image onto fabric, transfer the image directly to the foam, then carve finely detailed stamps. See Shelly's fabric on page 102.

Photocopy Transfers Using Iron-ons

Iron-on transfers originated in the T-shirt industry as a means of personalizing clothing. It is now possible to go into a copy shop and have a transfer printed to take home and apply yourself. Drawings, photographs, actual objects, and computer-generated imagery can all be printed onto heat-sensitive transfer paper.

The process is simple. Choose pictures from the sources around you. Color photographs work as well as original artwork—anything you can lay flat on the glass of the copy machine can be turned into a transfer. This includes objects such as feathers, leaves, flowers, crocheted doilies, cloth—the possibilities are endless. The copy shop uses a special paper when they print your transfer. The paper is like regular paper stock, but it is coated with heat-sensitive plastic. The image is printed on the surface of the coating; then, when you take the copy home and iron it against fabric, the coating melts under the heat of the iron and transfers your picture.

Not all copy shops are capable of making iron-on transfers. Call shops in your area and inquire about transfers. If you cannot find a shop that makes transfers, you can order them through the mail. (See "Resources" on page 156.)

Put together pages of images before visiting the copy shop. If you keep pictures of similar things together—a sheet of birds, a sheet of flowers, etc.—you will have a library you can use again and again. These copies are not inexpensive, so make originals in advance. You can fill sheet after sheet without wasted blank spots.

Cut out pictures of things you might incorporate into a design, and glue the pictures onto an 8½" x 11" piece of paper with a gluestick. Leave a ¼"-wide margin around the edges of each image. Most copiers reduce an image. Gluing pictures too close to the edges may cause incomplete transfers later. Be sure to trim unwanted background around the original images; otherwise, you will have to trim every time you use a transfer. Store originals in file folders, labeled by subject, in an upright position.

Once you have transfers in hand, cut out the individual images. Even though the space surrounding the objects is clear, it can yellow on some fabrics or leave an obvious plastic finish around shapes where you might prefer not to have an edge. Trimming solves this problem. Don't worry about cutting out a shape exactly. Trimming fairly close to the perimeter of the shape should be enough. On heavier-weight and more textured fabrics, it may not be necessary to trim pictures so completely. The rougher texture of the cloth obscures the plastic edge.

Iron-on transfers work well on smooth, evenly woven natural and synthetic fabrics. Light-colored fabrics produce better results.

Hand wash fabric embellished with iron-on transfers or use the washing machine's gentle cycle. Dry cleaning can strip the color from transfers. If you are using fabric that requires dry cleaning, test a transfer first, choose another process, or spot clean.

Materials

Iron and ironing board
Iron-on images
Craft scissors

Fabric (prewashed, dried, and ironed)

Optional Materials

Pressing cloth

Procedure

1. Assemble your materials and prepare your work area. Turn the iron to the cotton (high) setting.
2. Stretch out the dry, ironed fabric on your ironing board.
3. Cut an image from the transfer paper if you have not already done so. (This process goes faster if you cut out all the pictures first.)
4. Position the transfer, image side down, on the fabric.
5. Iron over the transfer. Be careful not to move the transfer while you are ironing or it will smear. As you iron, count to 10 on a lightweight fabric and to 20 on a heavyweight fabric.
6. Gently peel up one edge of the transfer while it is hot. If the transfer is complete, peel the paper away entirely. Peel carefully, since the image can also be distorted while it is hot. If some of the image remains on the paper, pat the edge down and repeat step 5. Always peel the paper away while it is hot to avoid damaging the transferred image.
7. Transfers can be used only once. Throw away the paper backings.
8. Continue to apply transfers as your design demands. If you are covering a large area, protect earlier transfers with a pressing cloth; the hot iron can melt a transferred image.

Tips and Variations
for Transferring Photocopies Using Iron-ons

❖ To include letters or words, make a transparancy of your photocopy before making copies to use as transfers. Color trasparencies make great originals—the edges don't curl, and they last a long time.

❖ The background color will affect the colors of the transfer. Instead of ironing your transfer directly onto dark fabric, try ironing it onto silk habotai or a similar lightweight fabric. Cut the image from the silk (the edges won't fray because they are fused by the transfer's components) and use an iron-on fusible web or fabric glue to attach the image to the darker fabric.

. . . . For Inspiration . . . . . .

He's Got the Whole World in His Hands
by Jane Dunnewold, 1991, San Antonio, Texas. Color iron-on transfers on silk. Beaded and quilted. (Photo by Jane Dunnewold)

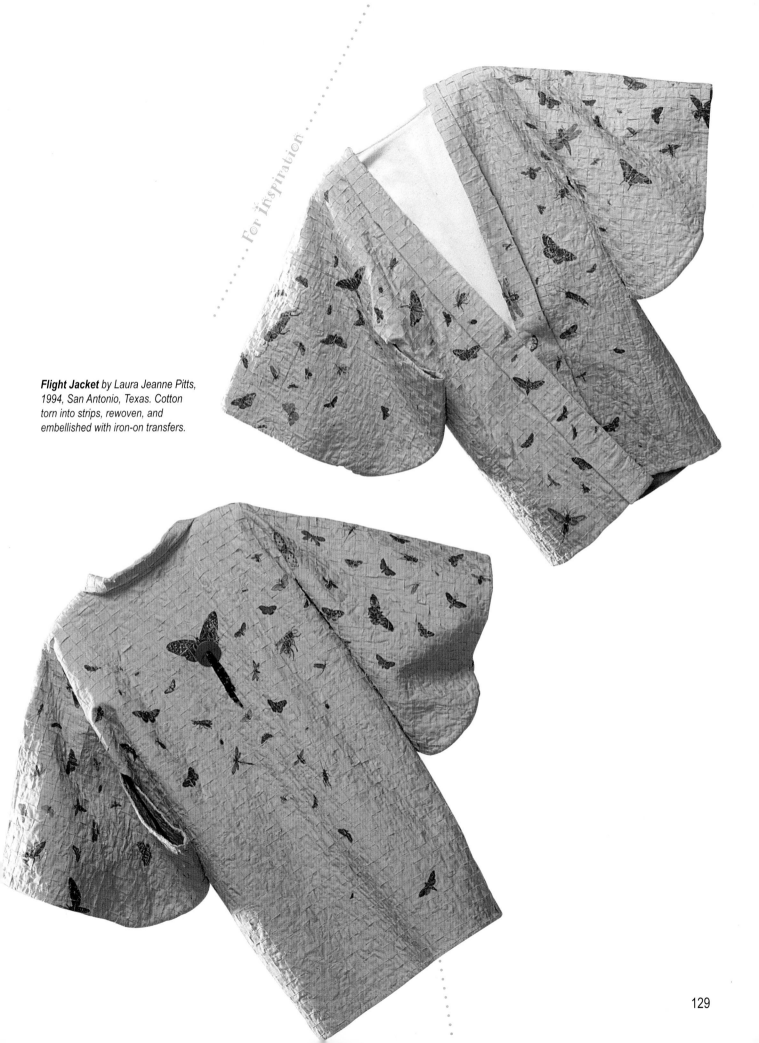

Flight Jacket by Laura Jeanne Pitts, 1994, San Antonio, Texas. Cotton torn into strips, rewoven, and embellished with iron-on transfers.

For inspiration

Photocopy Transfers Using Bondex Mending Tape

Margery Croner developed and perfected a method for transferring photocopy images using Bondex Mending Tape. She describes her method in *Fabric Photos.* (See "Bibliography" on page 155.) This process is a good alternative for those who don't want to expose themselves to solvents.

Bondex is a mending-tape product with a heat-sensitive adhesive back. It can be purchased in patches or in sheets. Bondex is sold in a variety of colors, but I recommend white for transfers.

This is a relatively simple process. You iron a piece of Bondex onto a black-and-white photocopy. When you peel away the Bondex, the ink on the copy transfers to the Bondex. Then, you iron the Bondex image onto the fabric. When you peel the Bondex away, the ink transfers to the fabric.

The success or failure of this process may depend on the copier you use. Different toners and inking systems affect the timing in the process as well as the clarity of the image. Make test copies and samples. Determine how long you should iron your copies to the mending tape and whether to peel while hot, warm, or cold. (See page 131.)

Bondex works well with smooth, evenly woven natural and synthetic fabrics. Light-colored fabrics produce better results. The glue residue left on the surface of the cloth may be more noticeable on some fabrics than on others and can yellow over time. Trim the image you have created if you want to be absolutely sure glue will not affect the look of the image later.

Fabric enhanced with mending-tape transfers can be hand or machine laundered or dry-cleaned.

Test

1. Copy a piece of black construction paper on the copy machine. The idea is to get a totally black copy.

2. Cut a 3" x 4" rectangle from the copy.

3. Using the cotton (high) setting on the iron, fuse a section of mending tape to the black copy. Do not push down on the iron during this step. Glide the iron across the surface of the tape.

Timing is critical. If you bear down on the iron and wait too long, the tape and the copy will permanently fuse. Try 10 seconds. If the two materials bond and cannot be separated, cut down the time and start your test again. If ink does not transfer to the mending tape, add 5-second increments to the ironing time until the transfer is clear.

4. When you finish counting, pull a third of the tape away from the paper. Do this while the paper is very hot. Wait a few seconds and pull away another third of the paper. When the paper is completely cool, peel away the last third.

The darkest of the three sections will indicate whether you should peel apart mending tape and paper while hot, warm, or cool.

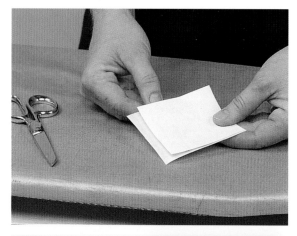

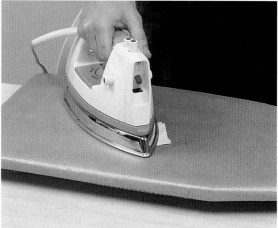

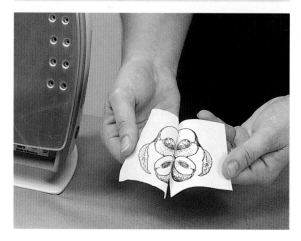

Materials

White Bondex Mending Tape
Black-and-white photocopy
Craft scissors

Iron and ironing board
Fabric (prewashed, dried,
    and ironed)

Optional Materials

Pressing cloth

Procedure

1. Assemble your materials and prepare your work area.
2. Cut a piece of Bondex slightly larger than the photocopy you are transferring. Trim both copy and mending tape to save materials
    It may be easier to peel away the paper if you leave a tab to grab onto after the two materials have been ironed together. This is especially true if you need to peel the two apart while they are still very hot.
3. Turn the iron to the cotton (high) setting.
4. Place the mending tape and photocopy right sides together, with the glue side of the mending tape facing the ink side of the photocopy.
5. Glide the iron over the mending tape and count. Use the count established in your testing.
6. Peel apart the mending tape and copy as determined in your testing. The photocopy image should have transferred to the mending tape. This image does not have to be used immediately; it can be saved and used later.
7. Stretch out the dry, ironed fabric on the work surface.
8. Position the transfer, image side down, on the fabric.
9. Press the transfer with the iron. Press down firmly this time and don't move the iron too much. If you are afraid your background fabric will scorch, use a pressing cloth under the iron. Count to 20 as you press.
10. Peel away the mending tape. Throw away the tape and paper backing.

Troubleshooting

Glide the iron on the first part of the transfer process. Bear down on the iron only during the second part of the process.

If you have trouble peeling apart the copy and the mending tape, you are either pushing too hard or heating too long.

Throw away the fused transfer and try again.

If the image is not transferring from the mending tape to the background, press both harder and longer. Still no luck? Try another copier.

Tips and Variations
for Transferring Photocopies Using Bondex

❖ Images transferred with Bondex are transparent. If desired, you can color these images with paint, colored pencils, or fabric markers. Color lightly to preserve the quality of the transferred image.

❖ Transfer a series of smaller images before attempting a larger transfer. To work with big pictures, cut them into components and apply the components separately.

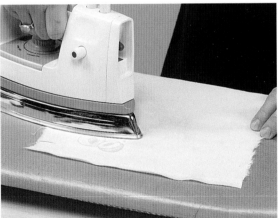

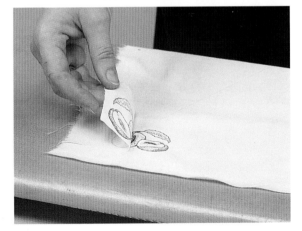

Just One Cup Before I Go by Alison Whittemore, 1994, San Antonio, Texas, 40" x 51". Hand-painted commercial fabrics with gel-medium transfers. Hand-colored photocopy. (Photo by Alison Whittemore)

Photocopy Transfers Using Gel Medium

Gel medium, which is available through art-supply stores, is an acrylic product used to build up the surface of an acrylic painting. Opaque when wet, it dries clear. Gel medium has a heavy consistency that greatly changes the hand of the fabric. Gel-medium transfers are best used as tiny accents or as a transfer medium on nonfunctional textile works.

Smooth, even-weave fabrics work best with these transfers. The photocopy must bond evenly or the image will tear away. The smoother the surface, the more reliable the bond. Since the color of the background fabric shows through the transfer, light fabrics work better than dark.

In addition to affecting the hand of the fabric, gel-medium transfers limit your choice of cleaning processes. Although the transfers are stable when dry, they become opaque and fragile when wet. Fabric enhanced with gel-medium transfers can be gently hand washed or dry-cleaned. Making several samples of the process should give you a better idea of how best to incorporate this technique into your complex cloths.

Gel-medium transfers can be cut out and used as applied embellishment or incorporated into a larger overall design scheme.

Materials

Plastic sheeting or a plastic
  garbage bag
Fabric (prewashed, dried,
  and ironed)
Gel medium
Plastic spoon
Shallow container

Foam brush
Black-and-white or color
  photocopies*
Brayer (a small rubber roller
  available at art-supply stores)
Dishpan or basin large enough to
  accommodate the fabric

Optional Materials

Iron and ironing board

Pressing cloth

Some magazine pictures will transfer, but if the paper is too glossy, the pictures probably won't adhere properly.

Procedure

1. Assemble your materials and prepare your work area. The gel medium will completely saturate the fabric. To protect your work area, cover it with plastic sheeting or a plastic garbage bag.
2. Stretch out the dry, ironed fabric on the work surface.
3. Spoon several dollops of gel medium into a shallow container.

4. Using the foam brush, coat the front of the photocopy with gel medium. The gel application should be smooth and thick. Keep the gel on the ink side of the photocopy only. If you get the gel on the back of the copy, it will seal the image to your work surface and make it impossible to remove.

5. Place the photocopy, gel side down, on the fabric.

6. Using the brayer, roll over the entire surface of the photocopy. Press down as you roll, smoothing out air bubbles, so the gel image adheres to the fabric. Do not add more gel medium at this point.

7. Carefully turn the fabric over. Using the brayer, roll over the fabric side of the transfer.

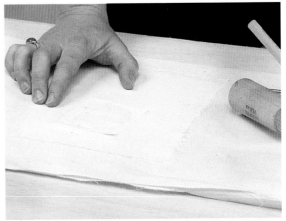

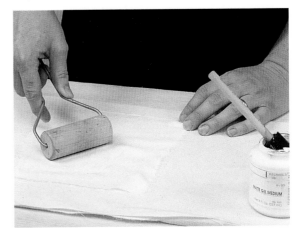

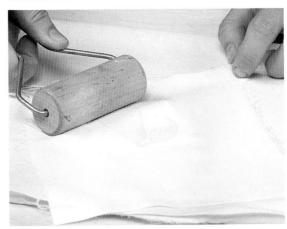

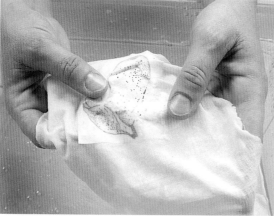

8. Allow the gel medium to dry 3 to 24 hours. The longer you wait, the more reliable your results. The gel *must* be dry before you proceed.

9. When the gel medium is completely dry, fill the dishpan with cool water. Immerse the fabric in the water and soak for 10 minutes. The paper will begin to soften and dissolve.

10. Remove the fabric from the water and gently rub the paper side of the photocopy with your thumb and fingers. The paper will begin to peel away. Continue to rub until the image becomes clearly visible.

The image is most fragile while you are removing the paper. If you rub too hard, some of the picture may rub away. If you do not rub enough, a hazy residue of paper fuzz will be visible when the fabric dries. If this happens, immerse the fabric again and finish rubbing away the remaining residue.

11. When you are sure the paper backing has been entirely rubbed away, allow the image to dry. The fabric may curl slightly during the drying time. You can iron the image after it has dried. Use a pressing cloth, since the gel can be softened by the iron's heat.

If you find a paper residue when the fabric dries, try applying a thin overcoat of gel medium. The gel medium will penetrate the remaining paper fiber and make it less visible (translucent).

12. Clean your tools immediately with soap and water. Gel medium cannot be removed after it dries.

Tips and Variations
for Transferring Photocopies Using Gel Medium

❖ You can color gel-medium transfers using fabric paint, colored pencils, or fabric markers. You may want to consider the cleaning requirements when choosing the coloring method.

❖ You can also transfer images from color magazines; however, heavy paper stock with a glossy finish will not transfer easily. The finish inhibits the transfer process. Images on newspaper and less-expensive stocks transfer nicely.

Someone's in the Kitchen with Satan's Minions
by Alison Whittemore, 1994, San Antonio, Texas, 37" x 48".
Hand-painted fabrics with gel-medium transfers. (Photo by
Alison Whittemore)

Decals Using Gel Medium

By changing the way you apply the gel-medium transfer, you can create a freestanding decal for use on fabric, wood, or glass.

Materials

Gel medium
Plastic spoon
Shallow container
Foam brush

Magazine page or photocopy
Dishpan or basin large enough to
    accommodate fabric

Optional Materials

Iron and ironing board

Pressing cloth

Procedure

1. Assemble your materials and prepare your work area.
2. Spoon several dollops of gel medium into a shallow container.
3. Using the foam brush, apply a smooth coating of gel medium to the front of the magazine page or photocopy. If you get gel medium on the back of the image, it will seal the image to your work surface and make it impossible to remove the paper. Make all the brush strokes in the same direction.
4. Wait for the gel medium to dry, then repeat step 3, brushing the second layer of gel onto the image in the opposite direction. Repeat this process, applying gel medium in alternating directions as each layer dries. The image should be coated at least 6 times, preferably 12. The more layers you apply, the stronger the final decal.
5. Allow the final coat to dry at least 24 hours.
6. Immerse the decal in cool water and soak for 10 minutes to soften the paper backing.
7. Gently rub the paper backing with your thumb and fingers. The paper will begin to peel away. Continue to rub the paper until the image becomes clearly visible.

    The image is at its most fragile while you are removing the paper. If you rub too hard, it may rub away. If you do not rub enough, a hazy residue of paper fuzz will be visible when the decal dries.
8. The decal may curl as it dries. Cover it with a pressing cloth and iron (low heat) to flatten.
9. Use gel medium to apply the decal to the background surface you have in mind. Once the image is dry, you can embellish it as desired.
10. Clean your tools immediately with soap and water. Gel medium cannot be removed after it dries.

Innocence by Jane Dunnewold, 1992, San Antonio, Texas, 14" x 17" x 2". Dyed, discharged, and painted rayon and cotton. Solvent transfer. Foiled, beaded, and embroidered. At right, detail of "Innocence." (Photo by Jane Dunnewold)

Emily's Lament *by Victoria von Koeppen, 1995, San Antonio, Texas, 50" x 60". Dyed and overdyed linen treated with a water-based resist. Hand painted, silk-screened, stamped, and embroidered.*

Many of the pieces of complex cloth you create are complete as soon as you finish the last process. This is especially true if you worked on yardage with a specific goal in mind—a garment for a special occasion or pillows for the house. Further enhancement may not be needed, or you may choose to wait until the project is under way before adding stitching or beading.

For other lengths of cloth, embroidery and beading are the "icing on the cake," taking them the extra distance from finished to spectacular. Even simple stitches look terrific when sewn with metallic or rayon thread and a glittering bead or two. The extra work can make a big difference.

Embroidery

If you do not have well-honed embroidery skills, start with the easiest stitches. I have included a few to get you started. (See "Bibliography" on page 155 for additional embroidery sources.) Embroidery is easy to learn, and you don't have to use the most complicated stitches or know loads and loads of them for the results to look great. And once you learn how, embroidery is fun.

Needlework shops and craft stores carry a large selection of beautiful threads in a rainbow of colors and styles. These threads enhance even the simplest of stitches. Avoid six-strand embroidery floss; it tangles when not separated properly and, let's face it, it's downright boring compared to other thread choices. Choose the jazzy, subtle, or multicolored strands that shout at you from the shelves. If you love the threads you're using, it will show in the finished product.

As you work, scale the weight of the threads to the weight of your fabric. Heavy threads are unsuitable and could actually damage lightweight fabric. Wispy, delicate threads can get lost on a heavy fabric. Avoid threads with slubs; they are meant for knitting and crochet.

Also scale the eye of the needle to the size of the thread. Too small an eye will make you crazy every time you try to thread it. Thread larger than the needle's eye will easily shred and result in a great deal of waste. Embroidery stitches are usually worked with embroidery needles—thin and sharp with large eyes. Tapestry needles are another choice. However, these needles have a blunt tip that makes it hard to stitch tightly woven fabric.

You will need a small embroidery hoop to keep your work taut. A 5" or 6" hoop is a good size. If you decide to work larger, consider an embroidery frame on a stand. It frees your hands and makes it easier to work big. Needlework stores carry a nice selection of embroidery frames in many price ranges.

. . . . For inspiration . . . .

Kitchen Meditation by Jane Dunnewold, 1995, San Antonio, Texas, 22" x 22". Hand-painted cotton and rayon. Silk-screened and beaded. Embellished with safety pins.

Embroidery Stitches

Materials
■ ■ ■ ■ ■ ■

Complex cloth
Assorted threads
Needles

Scissors
Small embroidery hoop

Optional Materials

Swing-arm lamp for lighting your
work area

Cross-Stitch

Cross-stitches can be made singly and do not need to be perfectly even. Consider making some of the stitches longer than others and varying the slope of the crossbars. This stitch is most interesting when worked in a variety of thread colors and stitch lengths.

1. Working from right to left, come up at A, go down at B, then come up at C. Go down at D and continue, making a series of slanting stitches. Keep the needle vertical.

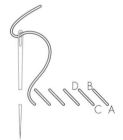

2. Reverse direction, working from left to right. Keep the needle vertical and pass it back through the holes made by the first set of stitches. This will form a row of cross-stitches.

French Knot

French knots can be done individually or in a group. Use thicker thread for larger knots.

1. Bring the needle up at A; wrap the thread around the needle once as shown. (Wrapping the needle more than once results in a floppy knot.)

2. Put the needle in at A (or just beside it) and slide the wrap down flush against the surface of the fabric. Don't wrap too tightly or it will be hard to pull through. Pull the needle through the hole.

3. If a finished knot has been completed correctly, it will sit right on the surface of the cloth.

Chain Stitch

Use this stitch individually or in a line. It is good for outlining or filling a shape.

1. Bring the needle up at A.

2. Form a loop and put the needle back in at A, holding the loop down with your finger. Come up at B, below A and *inside* the loop you have formed. Pull the needle through at B, creating the first stitch.

3. Repeat steps 1 and 2. Always insert the needle where the thread came up and make the second part of the stitch inside the next loop.

Couching

Use couching for outlining or filling a shape. Try contrasting colors and as many different threads as you like.

1. Smooth together 1 or more threads and lay them along the stitching line. (This may be an imaginary line, or you can draw a line with a disappearing marker.) Bring a needle threaded with 1 strand up at A. Go down at B, making a small stitch that will anchor the loose threads in place.

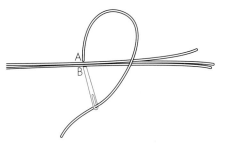

2. Take your next couching stitch ¼" away from A/B. Continue along the length of the thread, holding the loose threads taut with one hand.

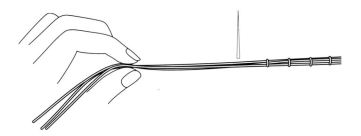

3. When you have finished couching, thread the loose top threads through a large-eye needle. Pass them through to the back of the cloth and make a knot, cutting off any excess thread. Repeat at the beginning of the loose threads.

Tips and Variations for Embroidery

❖ Dip-dye white rayon, silk, or cotton thread in an immersion dyebath to match your fabric. (See pages 55–56.) Use a gloved hand to dip the threads into the dye, or put them in a stocking and immerse. Batch and wash out according to instructions. Presto—designer threads!

❖ Stitch with 2 lightweight strands threaded through the needle together.

❖ Add basic stitching to your complex cloth, then cut out the garment you intend to make and add heavier, more complicated stitching when you know where the emphasis on the garment will be (front panel, lapels, etc.). It's easier to do the stitching before you assemble the garment.

Untitled Jacket by Susie Hettleman, 1994, Austin, Texas. Shibori-dyed silk noil. Embroidered and beaded.

For inspiration

For inspiration

Untitled Coat (above) by Susie Hettleman, 1993, Austin, Texas. Shibori-dyed silk. Discharged, embroidered, and beaded.

Investment Series (right) by Rachel Edwards, 1994, San Antonio, Texas. Iron-on color transfers. Hand stamped and airbrushed.

Beading

Beading can be as simple or as complicated as you choose. We are fortunate to be in the midst of a beading boom, which means you will find a huge selection to choose from. Most craft stores sell beads in small, inexpensive packages, making it affordable to stock up on several colors at once. Mail-order suppliers sell larger quantities of beads of all types and are the best choice if you need lots of one color or style.

If you are just beginning to add beads to your repertoire, follow the advice I offered on threads. Buy what you love when you see it—you may not be able to find a particular type or color again. And buy as many as you think you might need, then buy as many as you can afford! Stockpiling is a good idea; when you have a stash in your workroom, it is easier to decide what to use on the project at hand.

Strive for variety. Seed beads in all colors are always useful. Ethnic beads, stone beads, glass beads, and plastic beads—all will be useful eventually. Scout unexpected places, like garage sales and thrift stores, for savings on beads. You can often find old necklaces for a song. Take them apart and recycle the beads onto your complex cloth.

Think seriously about learning to make some kinds of beads yourself. Polymer clay beads are easy to make and can be created to match your fabric. You can make beads from paper, sheet metal, and found objects. Use your creativity and check "Resources" on page 156 for catalogs with beads and bead-making supplies

As for needles, scale these to fit the beads you are using. I prefer Betweens (quilting needles). These are available in a range of sizes, and small beads fit easily over a size 10 Between. Many stitchers prefer beading needles. These are very long and thin and bend easily, which drives me crazy. Try several needles and decide for yourself. The only real requirement is that the needle must easily pass through the bead.

Beading thread is not available in all colors. Choose a color related to your cloth or use perle cotton, sewing thread, or other thin embroidery thread. Do not use metallic or rayon threads; these have a tendency to break and shred. Choose a more stable thread when sewing down beads.

There are two common methods used to sew beads to cloth. Only the stitches vary. The preparation, beginning, and result are the same.

Sewing Beads to Cloth

Materials

Assorted beads (seed, ethnic, glass, wood, etc.)

Small dishes or containers for beads

Beading thread

Needles

Scissors

Complex cloth

FrayCheck™

Optional Materials

Beeswax (to strengthen the thread)

Procedures

1. Pour the beads you will be using into small containers.
2. Cut a piece of thread 15" to 18" long. I know it's tempting, but try not to work with too long a thread. It will tangle.
3. Thread the needle, then knot one end of the thread. Most of the time you will use a single strand of thread rather than a double.
4. Bring the thread up through the fabric from the back, at the place you will begin to bead; pull it tight.
5. Choose one of the following stitches.

BACKSTITCH (ONE BEAD AT A TIME)

This stitch is essentially "one step forward, two steps back." Always go down in the hole next to the bead you added last. Always come up one bead length to the left of the last bead you added. This stitch is very strong—a good way to sew beads to a garment.

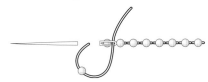

1. Thread a bead onto your needle and slide it down against the cloth.
2. Put the point of the needle into the fabric so the stitch is 1 bead length long, just to the right of where you brought the needle out of the cloth.
3. Bring the needle up 1 bead length to the left of the first bead. Add a bead to the thread, slide it down to the cloth, and put the point of the needle into the hole to the right of the bead you just added.
4. Bring the needle up 1 bead length to the left of the second bead and continue stitching.

A variety of embroidery stitches can be adapted for use with beads.

RUNNING STITCH (MORE THAN ONE BEAD AT A TIME)

Use this stitch to sew more than one bead at a time. Adjust your stitch length to accommodate the number of beads. Taking stitches shorter than the equivalent length of the beads on your thread will create an arch or loop—a variation you may enjoy.

You can also use this stitch to add individual beads in a scattered fashion. Try not to trail long lengths of thread across the back of the cloth, since it can catch and pull out or break.

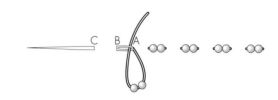

1. Thread a bead onto your needle and slide it down against the cloth.
2. Take a stitch 1 bead length long to the left of where the thread came up through the cloth.
3. Bring the needle up as close as possible to the left of the first bead.
4. Add another bead, slide it down against the cloth, and take 1 bead-length stitch to the left.
5. Continue adding beads. In the running stitch, you are always moving to the left. You never backstitch to the right. This is a weaker stitch that can catch and pull out if not sewn securely.
6. To end, return the needle to the back side of the cloth. Take several tiny stitches through 1 or 2 threads of the cloth, right under a bead. Put a drop of FrayCheck on the knot and trim the excess thread.
7. Continue sewing by rethreading your needle and repeating the steps above.

Tips and Variations for Beading

❖ Thread 5 or more beads onto your thread and take a stitch the equivalent length of 2 beads. When you pull the thread tight, you will make small loops of beads on the cloth surface. Double your thread if you want to use this variation on clothing—it will make the stitch stronger.

❖ Add a bead or two to embroidery stitches as you sew. For example, add a bead, make a cross-stitch. This is faster than splitting the techniques and completing them separately, and it integrates the beads into the stitching.

❖ If you are adding beads to a piece of cloth for a garment, stick to seed beads. You can add bigger decorative beads later, when you can strategically position them. No one wants to sit on a lumpy bead that just happened to end up on the seat of a garment!

❖ Consider cleanability. Seed beads can usually withstand washing and dry cleaning. Larger beads may not fare as well. If in doubt, test your beads.

❖ Dye unfinished wooden beads to match your cloth. Put the beads in a stocking along with a stone to sink them and place in an immersion bath (pages 55–56). No need to batch—they will be permanently colored when you remove them from the dye. Beads may dry lighter than they look when wet. Adjust the time in the dyebath accordingly.

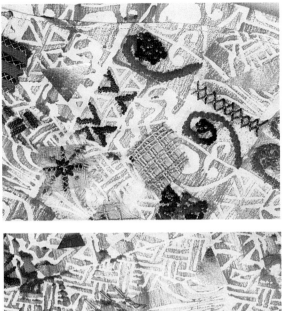

Family Armor by Victoria von Koeppen, 1994, San Antonio, Texas. Dyed and overdyed silk collar. Constructed and embroidered.

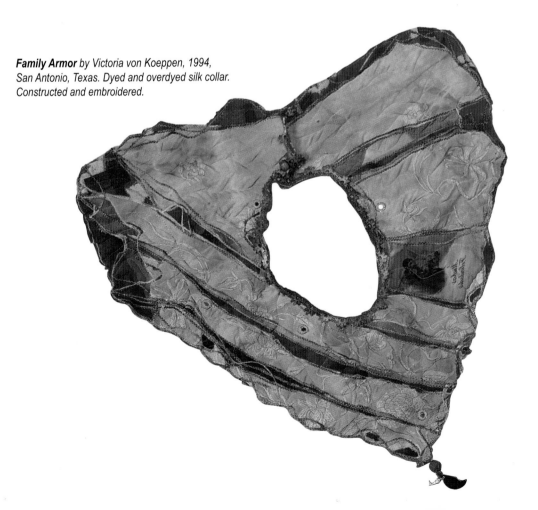

For inspiration

Tumbling Blocks *by Jane Dunnewold, 1996, San Antonio, Texas, 48" x 60". Dyed cotton and interfacing.*
Hand painted, silk-screened, puff-painted, and foiled.

Studies and Explorations

The information in this book may seem overwhelming at first. Complex cloth involves making many choices. It is a good idea to organize your thinking (and your studio) before you get started.

Begin by making samples of the processes described in each chapter. When you think of other ideas, make samples of them too. Label everything. A laundry pen allows you to write directly on most cloth, and adhesive labels give you a clear, consistent means of labeling any fabric. Use a gluestick to mount the samples in a notebook, or sew a buttonhole in the corner of each sample and thread samples onto ring binders. The visual reference you are creating is invaluable. You will refer to it often when you ask "What do I do now?" or "What did I do then?"

The following projects are drawn from a class I teach. Use them as a jumping-off point for your own studies and explorations. All the projects follow a similar format. Read the entire project before beginning and follow the instructions carefully. The end result may be affected if you make changes. For example, each project includes fabric guidelines for the techniques in that project. In an exercise using bleach, fabric content is very important. Using a polyester blend can be very disappointing.

I recommend working with a 2-yard length of fabric. This is long enough to be worthwhile if you want to make something from the fabric, but not so long that it is hard to manipulate. If you want to produce longer pieces, consider working in sections. Three or four sections, each 2 yards long, are much more manageable than one 6-yard length.

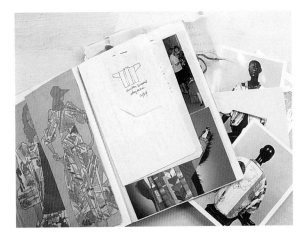

Color schemes are suggested to encourage you to learn more about color theory. If the color terminology used in a project doesn't mean anything to you, review "Color" on pages 16–18. Studying color and learning the language strengthens the designs you create. It may be intimidating, but stick with it. Choosing colors and understanding how they interact can become second nature. It just takes practice.

The projects are organized based on which techniques are best accomplished at the beginning, which can be used throughout a project, and which should be saved until a piece is nearly complete. As you work through the projects, think about the techniques you are using and how they relate to other techniques you could use. Making complex cloth and thinking about how these techniques relate will help you answer "What do I do next?"

Project 1
Guidelines

Fabric: 2 yds. cotton or rayon (Do not use synthetic blends or silk.)
Color scheme: Analogous or complementary

Steps

1. Dye the fabric in an immersion dyebath, following the instructions on pages 55–56. Do not manipulate (fold, pleat, etc.) the fabric.
2. Discharge the fabric with household bleach, following the instructions for one of the techniques (stamping, stenciling, etc.) on pages 66–73.
3. Overdye the discharged fabric in an immersion dyebath. Do not manipulate the fabric.
4. Stamp the fabric, using one color of fabric paint and following the instructions on pages 78–79.
5. Silk-screen the fabric, using a second color of fabric paint and following the instructions on pages 82–85.
6. Embellish the fabric with metallic foil, following the instructions for one of the techniques on pages 112–15.

Project 2
Guidelines

Fabric: 2 yds. cotton or rayon (Do not use synthetic blends or silk.)
Color scheme: Your choice

Steps

1. Pleat or fold the fabric and dye it in an immersion dyebath, following the instructions on pages 55–56.
2. Overdye the fabric in a different color (a second immersion dyebath). Do not manipulate the fabric before dyeing.
3. Silk-screen a design on the fabric, using 1 color of fabric paint and following the instructions on pages 82–85.
4. Silk-screen the same design on the fabric, using a second color of fabric paint.
5. Stamp the fabric, using a third color of fabric paint or metallic foil and following the instructions for one of the techniques on pages 78–79 for fabric paint or pages 112–13 for metallic foil.

Project 3
Guidelines

Fabric: 2 yds. cotton, rayon, or silk (Lightweight weave is preferred.)
Color scheme: Your choice

Steps

1. Silk-screen a design on the fabric, using a water-based resist and following the instructions on pages 82–84.
2. Once the resist has dried, use a PreVal Sprayer or plant mister to mist thinned fabric paint on the fabric, following the instructions on page 106. When the paint is dry, wash out the resist. Dry the cloth.
3. Overdye the fabric in an immersion dyebath. Do not manipulate the fabric before dyeing.
4. Using fabric paint, silk-screen the same design on the fabric.
5. Using a second color of fabric paint, silk-screen the same design on the fabric.
6. Embellish the design with embroidery, following the instructions on pages 142–44.

Project 4
Guidelines

Fabric: 2 yds. Cotton or rayon (Do not use synthetic blends.)
Color scheme: Monchromatic

Steps

1. Stuff the fabric into a nylon stocking and place in an immersion dyebath, following the instructions on pages 55–56.
2. Choose a technique for applying a water-based resist. (See "Using Water-Based Resists with Bleach" on pages 102–105.) Apply the resist to the fabric.
3. Once the resist has dried, use a PreVal Sprayer or plant mister to mist household bleach on the fabric. Wash and dry the fabric before proceeding.
4. Overdye the fabric in an immersion dyebath. Do not manipulate the fabric before dyeing.
5. Stamp the fabric, using 1 color of fabric paint and following the instructions on pages 78–79.
6. Using a second color of fabric paint (and pattern if desired), stamp the fabric again.

Project 5
Guidelines

Fabric: In this project, use 2 yds. of any fabric you like, including blends. Consider fabric with a woven design, such as a brocade or small woven check.

Color scheme: Light neutral (white, cream, beige)

Steps

1. Silk-screen a design on the fabric, using white fabric paint and following the instructions on pages 82–84.
2. Using cream fabric paint, silk-screen the same design over the white paint.
3. Using a pastel fabric paint, silk-screen the same design on the fabric.
4. Using white puff paint, silk-screen accents on the fabric.
5. *Optional:* Using brightly colored fabric paint, stamp a small element, such as a square, triangle, or squiggle, or apply a small foiled accent, using fusible web.

Project 6
Guidelines

Fabric: In this project, use 2 yds, of any fabric you like, including blends. A woven design is desirable.

Color scheme: Light neutral (white, cream, beige, pastels)

Steps

1. Silk-screen a design on the fabric, using white fabric paint and following the instructions on pages 82–84.
2. Using a pastel fabric paint, silk-screen a different design on the fabric.
3. Tear the fabric into 2"- to 4"-wide strips.
4. Sew the strips together again, rearranging them if desired. Or sew the strips together so the seams are on the right side of the fabric length.
5. Using white fabric paint, silk-screen the design in step 2 on the fabric.
6. Using fabric paint, stencil a small accent in a darker version of the pastel used in step 2.

Project 7
Guidelines

Fabric: 2 yds. black cotton or rayon (Do not use synthetic blends or silk, and prewash the fabric.)

Color scheme: This project revolves around the discharging process. Choose the dye colors based on the color of your fabric after it has been discharged.

Steps

1. Pleat, fold, or bunch the fabric.
2. Place the fabric in a bucket and pour household bleach over it. Remove the fabric as soon as it discharges.
3. Wash and dry the fabric, following instructions on page 72.
4. Overdye the fabric in an immersion dyebath, following the instructions on pages 55–56.
5. Discharge the fabric, using bleach and following the instructions for stamping on page 66 or stenciling on page 67.
6. *Optional:* Overdye the fabric in another immersion dyebath.

Project 8
Guidelines

Fabric: 2 yds. black cotton or rayon (Do not use synthetic blends or silk, and prewash the fabric.)

Color scheme: Achromatic (black and variations; no true hue)

Steps

1. Discharge the fabric, using household bleach and following the instructions for stamping on page 66.
2. Overdye the fabric in an immersion dyebath, using brown or gray fiber-reactive dye and following the instructions on pages 55–56.
3. Discharge the fabric, using bleach and a large stencil pattern, and following the instructions for stenciling on page 67. Be sure to wash and dry the fabric before continuing.
4. Apply a wash of thinned fabric paint. You can brush or spray on the fabric paint. As an option, apply the paint in spots so that previously dyed sections of the cloth remain.
5. Embellish the fabric with metallic foil, following the instructions for one of the techniques on pages 112–15.

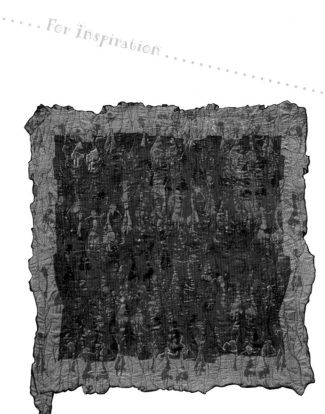

Spirit Dancers: Fire (above) by Beth Kennedy, 1994, Austin, Texas, 48" x 50". Dyed and overdyed cottons. Silk-screened and foiled. Machine-embroidered.

Project 9
Guidelines

Fabric: 2 yds. silk, rayon, or cotton (The fabric must have a smooth, even weave.)

Color scheme: Bright (tropicals, primaries, complements)

Steps

1. Stuff the fabric into a nylon stocking and place it in an immersion dyebath, following the instructions on pages 55–56.
2. After washing the fabric, stuff the fabric back into the stocking and overdye it in another immersion dyebath, using a complementary color. (For example, if the first dyebath was turquoise, use orange for the second dyebath.) Batch, wash, and dry the fabric after dyeing.
3. Choose a large, open, black-and-white image you can transfer. Following the instructions for one of the photocopy transfer techniques on pages 122–33, apply an overall pattern.
4. Using thick or thin fabric paint, hand color the black-and-white images.
5. *Optional:* If your color scheme is a pale to medium value, use color iron-on transfers as accents. If your color scheme is a medium to dark value, use metallic foil accents.

Project 10
Guidelines

Fabric: 2 yds. silk, rayon, or cotton (The fabric must have a smooth, even weave.)

Color scheme: Your choice

Steps

1. Fold, pleat, or stuff the fabric into a nylon stocking and place it in an immersion dyebath, following the instructions on pages 55–56.
2. After washing the fabric, fold, pleat, or stuff it back into the stocking and overdye it in another immersion dyebath, using an analogous color. Batch, wash, and dry the fabric.
3. Silk-screen a random pattern, using fabric paint that matches one of the dye colors and following the instructions on pages 82–85.
4. Using fabric paint that matches the second dye color, silk-screen the same pattern.
5. Silk-screen glue, following the instructions for silk screening fabric paint. Wait for the glue to dry, then apply gold or silver metallic foil.
6. Using metallic gold or silver beads, bead the fabric in a random pattern.

Bibliography

Adachi, Fumi. *Japanese Design Motifs.* New York: Dover Publications, Inc., 1972.

Albers, Joseph. *The Interaction of Color.* New Haven, Conn.: Yale University Press, 1963.

Allen, Jeanne. *Designer's Guide to Japanese Patterns.* San Francisco: Chronicle Books, 1984.

Bang, Molly. *Picture This: Perception and Composition.* Boston, Mass.: Bulfinch Press, 1991.

Bates, Kenneth F. *Basic Design.* Cleveland: World Publishing Company, 1960.

Bosker, Gideon, Michele Mancini, and John Gramstad. *Fabulous Fabrics of the '50s.* San Francisco: Chronicle Books, 1992.

Bothwell, Dorr, and Marlys Mayfield. *Notan: The Dark-Light Principle of Design.* New York: Dover Publications, Inc., 1991.

Christie, Archibald. *Pattern Design.* New York: Dover Publications, Inc., 1969.

Croner, Marjorie. *Fabric Photos.* Loveland, Colo.: Interweave Press, 1989.

Enthoven, Jacqueline. *The Stitches of Creative Embroidery.* New York: Van Nostrand Reinhold, Inc., 1974.

Fanning, Robbie. *Decorative Machine Stitchery.* New York: Butterick Publishing, 1976.

Gaber, Susan. *Treasury of Flower Designs.* New York: Dover Publications, Inc., 1981.

Howell-Koehler, Nancy. *Photoart Processes.* Worchester, Mass.: Davis Publications, 1980.

Itten, Johannes. *The Art of Color.* New York: Van Nostrand Reinhold, Inc., 1961.

Karasz, Mariska. *Adventures in Stitches.* New York: Funk and Wagnalls Co., 1959.

Kleeberg, Irene. *The Butterick Fabric Handbook.* New York: Butterick Publishing, 1975.

Lauer, David. *Design Basics.* New York: Holt, Reinhart and Winston, 1979.

Laury, Jean Ray. *Imagery on Fabric.* Lafayette, Calif.: C & T Publishing, 1992.

Mayer, Anita Luvera. *Hands That Weave.* Loveland, Colo.: Interweave Press, 1984.

Menten, Theodore. *Japanese Border Designs.* New York: Dover Publications, Inc., 1975.

Midolle, Silvestre, et al. *Florid and Unusual Alphabets.* New York: Dover Publications, Inc., 1976.

Nesbitt, Alexander. *Decorative Alphabets and Initials.* New York: Dover Publications, Inc., 1959.

The New Quilt 2. Dairy Barn Quilt National. Newtown, Conn.: The Taunton Press, 1993.

Phillips, Peter, and Gillian Bunce. *Repeat Patterns.* London: Thames and Hudson, 1993.

Porcella, Yvonne. *A Colorful Book.* Modesto, Calif.: Porcella Studios, 1986.

Proctor, Richard, and Jennifer Lew. *Surface Design for Fabric.* Seattle, Wash.: University of Washington Press, 1984.

———. *The Principles of Pattern.* New York: Van Nostrand Reinhold, Inc., 1971.

Schwalbach, Matilda, and James Schwalbach. *Silk-Screen Printing for Artists and Craftsmen.* New York: Dover Publications, Inc., 1970.

Scott, Joyce. *Fearless Beadwork.* Rochester, N.Y.: Visual Studies Workshop, 1994. (To order this book, write to: Visual Studies Workshop, 31 Prince Street, Rochester, NY 14607.)

Visions Quilts: Layers of Excellence. Quilt San Diego. Lafayette, Calif.: C & T Publishing, 1994.

Waterman, Ann V. *Design Your Own Repeat Patterns.* New York: Dover Publications, Inc., 1986.

Williams, Geoffrey. *African Designs from Traditional Sources.* New York: Dover Publications, Inc., 1971.

Wilson, Erica. *Erica Wilson's Embroidery Book.* New York: Charles Scribner's Sons, 1973.

Resources

Createx, Inc.
14 Airport Road
East Granby, CT 06026
1-800-243-2712
Free price lists and product-information flyers. Fabric paints, dyes, and metallic foils.

Dharma Trading Company
Box 150916
San Rafael, CA 94915
1-800-542-5227
Free catalog. Large selection of dyes, paints, and related products.

Dick Blick
Box 1267
Galesburg, IL 61402
1-800-447-8192
Free catalog. Large selection of art supplies, dyes, and paints.

Hues, Inc.
1-317-642-5666
Photo Effects™ heat-sensitive transfer paper.

Jones Tones®
68-743 Perez Road, Suite D-16
Cathedral City, CA 92234
1-800-397-9667 or Fax 1-619-770-9042
Photocopy transfers and metalic foils.

Nasco/Triarco
1-800-685-9361 or 1-800-558-9595
Safety-cut pliable stamping medium.

PROChemical & Dye, Inc.
Box 14
Somerset, MA 02726
1-508-676-3838 (information) or 1-800-2-BUY-DYE (ordering)
Free catalog. Dyes, paints, and related products.

Real Goods Trading Co.
555 Leslie Street
Ukiah, CA 95482
1-800-762-7325
Source for Citrisolve and other environment-friendly products.

Rupert, Gibbon, and Spider, Inc.
Box 452
Healdsburg, CA 95448
1-800-442-0455
Free catalog. Great fabrics for dyeing and painting as well as paints, dyes, and related products.

Screen-Trans Development Co.
100 Grand Street
Moonachie, NJ 07074
1-201-933-7800
The inventor of foils! Carries the best foil glue and a huge selection of foil colors and widths.

Testfabrics, Inc.
Box 420
Middlesex, NJ 08846
1-908-469-6446
Free catalog. Great fabrics for dyeing.

Texicolor Corporation, Inc.
444 Castro Street, Suite 400
Mountain View, CA 94041-2053
1-415-968-8183 or fax 415-969-8660
Free product list. All kinds of paints, including puffing medium for fabric paints. Large range of screening products.

Thai Silks
252F State Street
Los Altos, CA 94022
1-800-722-SILK or fax 1-415-948-3426
Price list or samples available. Large selection of silk fabrics at great prices.

Unisyn (Universal Synergetics)
16510 SW Edminston Road
Wilsonville, OR 97070
1-503-625-2323 or fax 1-503-625-4329
Free catalog. Terrific beads and beading supplies.

Welsh Products, Inc.
932 Grant Street
Benicia, CA 94510
1-800-745-3255
Puffing medium and quality paints.

Appendixes

Appendix A: Weights and Measures

Conversion Table

Liquid Measure	Volume Equivalents		
1 teaspoon	⅓ tablespoon	⅙ fluid ounce	4.9 milliliters
3 teaspoons	1 tablespoon	½ fluid ounce	14.8 milliliters
6 teaspoons	2 tablespoons	1 fluid ounce	29.6 milliliters
16 tablespoons	1 cup	8 fluid ounces	.237 liter
2 cups	1 pint	16 fluid ounces	.473 liter
2 pints	1 quart	32 fluid ounces	.946 liter
4 quarts	1 gallon	128 fluid ounces	3.785 liters

Solid Weight Equivalents

1 ounce		28.35 grams
16 ounces	1 pound	453.6 grams
2.2 pounds	1,000 grams	1 kilogram
100 grams	3.5 ounces	
10 grams	.35 ounce	
1 gram	1,000 milligrams	15.43 grains

Metric Fluid Capacity

10 milliliters	1 centiliter	.338 fluid ounce
100 milliliters	1 deciliter	3.38 fluid ounces
1,000 milliliters	1 liter	1.05 liquid quarts
10 liters	2.64 gallons	

Appendix B: Comparing Fabric Paints

Refer to "Resources" on page 156 for the addresses and phone numbers of the companies listed here.

Company Codes

CR	Createx
DH	Dharma Trading Company
L	Usually available locally
PC	PROChemical & Dye
T	Texicolor

Technique Codes

AP	Air pen
B	Brush
SP	Spray
SS	Silk screen
ST	Stamp

Company	Product	Use	Notes
PC/DH	Cloud Cover	B, SS, ST	Opaque. Good coverage on dark fabric.
PC/DH	Lumiere	B, SS, ST	Metallic. Good coverage on black fabric.
DH	Deka Print	B, SS, ST	Formulated for silk screening.
DH	Versatex Printing Paint	B, ST, SS	Formulated for silk screening.
DH	Versatex	AP, B, ST, SS	Formulated for airbrushing, but thick enough for other processes. Smooth finish.
DH	Deka Fabric Paint	B, ST, SS, AP	Very versatile. Not as opaque as other paints.
DH	Setacolor	B, ST, SS, AP	Thinner consistency than some other paints.
DH	Jacquard Textile Colors	B, ST, SS, AP	Very high quality. Minimal effect on the hand of the fabric.
DH	Starbright	B, ST	Do not silk screen; contains glitter.
DH	Peintex	B, ST, SP, AP	Watercolor consistency. Great colors
DH	Deka Silk Paints	B, ST, SP, AP	Misnamed. Good on all fabric types. Great colors. Watercolor consistency.
PC	Textile Ink	B, ST, SS, AP	Transparent base. Lost on dark colors. Very smooth.
PC	Opaque Textile Ink	B, ST, SS, AP	Good coverage on dark fabrics. Very opaque.
PC	Liquid Decorator Colors	B, ST, SP	Colors tend to fade.
CR	Poster/Fabric Paint	B, SS, ST	Very thick. Opaque.
CR	Pearlescents	B, SS, ST, AP	Great metallics. Fairly transparent.
CR	Pure Pigments	———	Pure Pigments are concentrated pigment. These must be added to a binding product—called a textile medium or base—before using or they will not adhere to the fabric.
CR	Textile Medium	B, SS, ST	Opaque or transparent. Best system for personal color mixing and value.
L	Ceramcoat	B, ST, SS	Inexpensive. Wide range of colors. No extra medium needed for fabric use.

Company	Product	Use	Notes
L	FolkArt	B, ST, SS	Inexpensive. Great metallics. Can dry quickly on a silk screen; exercise caution.
L	Apple Barrel	B, SS, ST	Inexpensive. Many colors. No extra medium needed for fabric use.
L	Liquitex	B, SS, ST	Acrylic paint for general use. Affects hand of fabric considerably. Dries quickly on a silk screen. Good metallics.
T	Fabric Paints	B, SS, ST	High quality. Very smooth. Transparent.
T	Screen Paints	SS, ST, B	Formulated for silk screening, but can be adapted for other uses.
T	Opaque Paints	B, SS, ST	Very opaque, good coverage.
L	Tulip Puff Paints	B, ST, SS	Tiny amounts. Expensive.
T	Puffing Agent	B, ST, SS	Add to paint. You control the amount. Intermixable with other brands.

Appendix C: Photocopy Processes at a Glance

Technique	Cleaning	Notes
Solvent transfer (black/white)	Wash or dry-clean.	Very durable. Can be hand colored or painted.
Solvent transfer (color)	Wash or dry-clean.	Skin tones may be garish when transferred. For photos, use iron-on.
Color iron-on transfer	Hand or gentle machine wash/dry-clean.	Dry cleaning may strip color image. Iron on the wrong side.
Bondex Mending Tape transfer	Wash or dry-clean.	Can be hand colored. Leaves a residue around image that may discolor. Trim to prevent.
Gel-medium transfer	Gentle hand wash.	Can be hand colored. Stiffens fabric.
Gel-medium decal	Gentle hand wash.	Stiffens fabric. Allows for the use of full color.

Index